Marriage facts before, during, and beyond

The Highest Human Relationship
what you should know

Dr. Maxine Lawrence

WESTBOW
PRESS
A DIVISION OF THOMAS NELSON

WestBow Press books may be ordered through booksellers or by contacting:

WestBow Press
A Division of Thomas Nelson
1663 Liberty Drive
Bloomington, IN 47403
www.westbowpress.com
1-(866) 928-1240

ISBN: 978-1-4497-8217-7 (sc)
ISBN: 978-1-4497-8218-4 (e)

Library of Congress Control Number: 2013900823

Printed in the United States of America

WestBow Press rev. date: 04/15/2013

Contents

Acknowledgments. vii

Introduction ix

Marriage the Highest Human Relationship: What
    You Should Know. 1

Marriage Is God's Idea 5

Unfaithfulness Breaks the Bond of Trust, the
    Foundation of All Relationships. 18

Taking Responsibility for Each Other's Welfare 29

Serious Road Blocks In Marriages. 51

Domestic Violence: What It Is, How to Stop It,and
    How to Recognize It before Marriage 71

The Effects of Divorce on Society: Government
    Neglect of Marriage 90

1994 Rank and Divorce Rates for Each State 96

What It Means to Fight for Your Marriage. 99

Dealing with Guilt and Shame 121

How to Survive Divorce on Biblical Grounds. 130

Why is forgiving important to Divorce Recovery?. 141

Moving from Divorce to Remarriage 143

What Does a Biblical Relationship Look Like? 155

Dating and Your Children. 161

Blended Families. 176

The Worst and Best Ways to Prepare for Marriage. 186

Summary 192

Conclusion 193

Notes. 196

Glossary 203

Bibliography 206

Acknowledgments

I thank the Lord Jesus Christ for impressing upon me the desire to publish this manual. To God be the glory for the great things He has done.

With great appreciation, I would like to thank my mother, Allie, and my father, Otis Ghant, for their courageous and godly impact on my life.

I especially appreciate Mama Bernice Toland for rearing and instructing me in the fear of the Lord.

A special, loving thank-you goes to my children: Richard Jr., Crystal, Joyya, and Emmanuel for bringing joy and growth into my life as a mother.

I also want to thank my sisters, Marilyn and Otie, and my brothers, Walter and Lionel.

I thank you, Stephanie, for the technical support of writing this manual. Also, I would like to thank Lisa Arceneaux for clerical assistance with the manual.

I give praise and thanks to Mom and Dad Hardy of the Bishop A. L. Hardy Academy of Theology in Seattle, Washington, for their directive to write this Manuel, my life will never be the same.

I also want to thank The Gresham Salvation Army, Majors James and Laura Sullivan, for their shared encouragement to pursue my passion of ministry, also Bishop Marcus and Dr. Jean Pollard of the COGIC United, and the many brothers and sisters in the body of Christ who have prayed for me to accomplish the will of God.

With my eternal gratitude,
Dr. Maxine Lawrence, D. Min.

Introduction

Due to a lack of information on many of life's issues, we as humans try to do the best we can with our given resources, often drawing from our own experiences, family of origin, or words of advice. As we look at the topic of marriage, the highest human relationship, we see much confusion and misinformation.

My friend has given me permission to share her story. She recalls: "Late one afternoon around 4:50 p.m., my son-in-law John called. Before I answered, I heard the Holy Spirit say, *Have a gentle tone when you say hello*. I heard the desperation and anxiety in John's voice on the other end as he said, 'Mom, it's me, John. I'm sorry I called you at work, but I had to talk to somebody. She's slipping away as the days pass. My wife doesn't want to be married anymore. Please pray. I've got to do something.' He and my daughter had only been married for a year.

"I drove to a nearby park and sobbed. My eyes were opened to the effect that my own divorce had had on my daughter. My daughter, being a college grad from an Ivy League institute, wanted out of her marriage, believing that divorce was the answer. Though pregnant, she believed she could manage on her own without the child's father. This truly was the day I saw how divorce can affect the next generation."

My friend had survived several divorces herself, and her daughter had absorbed the idea that if you don't like it, you get out. My friend has reported that, through much prayer and wise counsel, her daughter's attitude has changed, and the marriage is progressing well.

A growing number of people believe that annulment, separation, or divorce is the answer to marital problems. They have bought into Hollywood's version of marriage: the Cinderella-happy-ever-after life. Claiming that not all married people are joined together by God, they believe they are free to divorce—in order to marry the one God intended them to have. The fact is, God honors marriage and will hold people responsible for their vows.

The problem in our society is that the marriage covenant is not taken seriously, nor are marriage counseling and education valued or sought after, even though marriage is the primal relationship among humans.

It is my hope to equip those in the helping professions to educate both single and married individuals about God's original blueprint for marriage and its maintenance. It is my prayer that you will learn what the Scripture says on this subject and feel empowered to guide others toward the correct course of action in this critical area.

As the reader, you may be looking for wisdom in the area of marriage and family, and this book addresses marriage, divorce, and remarriage. Before you make any permanent decisions about your future in marriage, I suggest that you prayerfully read this book and consult a biblical counselor for the appropriate next steps you should take. Remember, your choices will affect the generations to come.

Dr. Maxine Lawrence

Marriage the Highest Human Relationship: What You Should Know

Marriage is the state in which a husband and wife live together in a sexual relationship with the approval of their social group.[1] The story of Adam and Eve describes the unique husband-wife relationship as "one flesh" (Genesis 2:18)[2] and illustrates the intimate relationship between God and his people (Hosea 1–3)[3] and between Christ and his church.

The most intimate of relationships among human beings is the husband-wife relationship, which is contrary to the belief of modern society that the parent-child relationship is the highest.

So, what does it mean to be married? Marriage is defined as a legal, blood-covenant union between a man and a woman who are wed in holy matrimony.

What makes the husband and wife relationship unique among human relationships? Many individuals do not realize that the husband-and-wife relationship is the highest human relationship—higher even than relationships between parent and child or among siblings, family, or friends.

Marriage is the relationship God designed for procreation. Only a male-female relationship can produce another human being. Think about that for a moment. Mankind was not the originator of marriage. The idea came from God, who said in Genesis 2:18: "It is not good that the man should be alone; I will make him an help meet for him."[4]

God went on to say in Genesis 2:24, "Therefore shall a man leave his father and mother and cleave unto his wife and the two shall become one flesh.[5]

What was God's Original Purpose for Marriage?

In his book about strengthening your marriage, author Wayne A. Mack says, "As far as I know, there is only one statement about marriage that God includes four times in the Bible."[6] He made it in Genesis 2:24,[7] Matthew 19:5,[8] Mark 10:7–8,[9] and Ephesians 5:31[10].

The statement is this: "For this cause shall a man leave his father and mother and shall cleave to his wife, and they shall become one flesh." God said it once in the Old Testament and three times in the New Testament. He said it once before man fell into sin and three times after man fell into sin. This statement contains God's all-time blueprint for a good marriage. A good design or blueprint is just as necessary for a successful marriage as it is for developing or building a project.

The problem we face today is in taking the marriage relationship for granted. We somehow think there's not much to making marriage work, as long as the emotional and sexual feelings are present. But when the difficult days emerge, the skies are overcast, and we don't feel that in-love feeling, a marriage not built on a covenant relationship won't stand.

God's blueprint design for marriage instructs husbands and wives to leave their fathers and mothers and to develop their own family.

What Does It Mean To Leave Your Parents?

What it does *not* mean is to utterly abandon or forsake them. (Observe Exodus 20:12,[11] Mark 7:9–13,[12] and 1 Timothy 5:8.[13])

Nor does it mean that you must make a great geographical move. Living too close to parents at the beginning of a marriage may make it more difficult to leave, but it is possible to leave your father and mother and still live next door. Conversely, it is possible to live a thousand miles away from your parents and not leave them. In fact, you may not have left your parents even though they are dead.

Leaving your parents means that you choose:

- To establish an adult relationship with them.
- To consider your mate's ideas, opinions, and practices above those of your parents.
- Not to be overly dependent on your parents' counsel, affection, assistance, and approval.
- To forgive the past mistakes of your parents. Otherwise you will be emotionally tied to them, no matter how far you move away.
- Not to change your mate simply to please your parents.

Because you are establishing a new family, you want to be more concerned with becoming a good husband or wife versus still being concerned with being a good son or daughter, aunt or uncle, grandson, and so forth.

If you are a parent, you should understand that it is critical for emotional growth that you prepare your children to leave. Staying will cripple them emotionally.

Many times when the so-called "empty nest syndrome" occurs, parents find that they have spent so much time investing in their relationship with their children that they, the husband and wife, don't know each other.

It is important also to note that when your children marry, you must not try to control their lives. Instead, encourage your daughter or son to depend upon her or his mate for guidance, help, affection, and companionship.

The Case for Early Marriage

Abstinence is not to blame for our marital crises, but promoting it has come at a cost in a permissive world where we are increasingly postponing marriage. The importance of Christian marriage as a symbol of God's covenantal faithfulness to his people—and a witness to the future union of Christ and his bride—will only grow in significance as the wider Western culture diminishes both the meaning and actual practice of marriage. Marriage itself will become a witness to the gospel.

I study romantic relationship formation. I've spoken with hundreds of young adults about not only what they think or hope for, but also what they actually do. Time and again, I've listened to Christian undergraduates recount to me how their relationships turned sexual.

One thing I never ask them is *why*. I *know* why: because sex feels great; it feels connectional; it feels deeply human. I never blame them for wanting that. Sex is intended to deepen personal relationships, and desire for it is intended to promote marriage. Such are the impulses of many young Christians in love. In an environment where parents and peers are encouraging them to delay thoughts of marriage, I'm not surprised that their sexuality remains difficult to suppress and is the source of considerable angst.

We would do well to recognize some of these relationships for what they are: marriages in the making. If a young couple displays maturity, faith, fidelity, a commitment to understanding marriage as a covenant, and a sense of realism about marriage, then it's our duty—indeed, our pleasure—to help them expedite the part of marriage that involves public recognition and celebration of what God is already knitting together. We ought to "rejoice and delight" in them and praise their love (Song of Solomon 1:4).[14]

Marriage Is God's Idea

In Genesis 2:18–24,[15] the Lord God said,

> It is not good for the man to be alone. I will make a helper suitable for him. Now the Lord God had formed out of the ground all the beasts of the field and all the birds of the air. He brought them to the man to see what he would name them; and whatever the man called each living creature, that was its name. So the man gave names to all the livestock, the birds of the air and all the beast of the field. But for Adam, no suitable helper was found. So God caused the man to fall into a deep sleep: and while he was sleeping, he took one of the man's ribs and closed up the place with flesh. Then the Lord God made a woman from the rib he had taken out of the man, and he brought her to the man. The man said, "This is now bone of my bones and flesh of my flesh, she shall be called "Woman," because she was taken out of man. For this reason a man will leave his father and mother and be united to his wife, and they will become one flesh.

Let's notice that God's creative work was not complete until he made woman. He could have made her from the dust of the ground, as he had made man. However, God chose to make her from the man's flesh (rib) and bone. In doing so, he illustrated that, in marriage, man and woman symbolically become one flesh. Notice this beautiful order: God gives life to man, man gives life to woman, and woman gives life to the world. God gave marriage as a *gift* to Adam and Eve. They were created perfectly for each other. Marriage was not created for convenience, nor was it brought about by any culture. It was instituted by God and has three basic aspects:

1. The man leaves his parents and, in a public act, promises himself to his wife.
2. The man and woman are joined together by taking responsibility for each other's welfare and by loving the mate above *all others*.
3. The two become one flesh in the intimacy and commitment of sexual union, which is reserved for marriage.

Marriages that are strong include all three of these aspects.

Commitment: Essential for a Successful Marriage

In Genesis 24:58–60[16], Rebekah's family asked her, "Will you go with this man?"

"I will go," she said.

So they sent their sister Rebekah on her way, along with her nurse and Abraham's servant and his men. And they blessed Rebekah and said unto her, "Our sister, may you increase to thousands upon thousands. May your offspring possess the gates of their enemies."

God intended marriage to be a lifetime commitment (Genesis 2:24).[17] When a person enters into marriage, divorce should not be an option for solving problems, nor a way out of a relationship that seems dead. *Commitment* is a word that many people run away from. Let's discover what this word means.

In the Greek, it is *parathithēmi*:[18] "to entrust, put forth, allege." A commitment is a covenant.[19] The Hebrew word is *bĕrît*: "a treaty, compact, agreement; to bind; an association between two parties with various responsibilities, benefits, and penalties."

The phrase "to cut a covenant is to make a covenant" refers to the act of ceremonially cutting an animal into two parts—with an implication of serious consequences for not fulfilling the covenant. In this sacred blood covenant, there are always two parties involved. The husband is to love his wife as Christ loved the church and gave himself for her. The commitment of the wife is to be exclusive, in total devotion to her husband.

The basic characteristic of a covenant is the idea of a "bond," according to the majority of scholars. A general characteristic of the Old Testament *bĕrît* is its unalterable and permanently binding character. "I will be their God and they shall be my people" (Jeremiah

11:4[20]; 24:7; 30:22; 32:38; Ezekiel 11:20; 14:11; 36:28; 37:23[21]; Zechariah 8:8.[22]).

The term *hesed* is used in the Old Testament to share God's motive in adopting the Israelites as his own "covenant children," indicating "loving kindness or covenant-love" (1 Samuel 20:8[23]).

Marriage, in relation to the term *covenant*, means two individuals—a man and woman—making, in a sense, the *hesed* covenant and promising each other, before God and witnesses, to fulfill their responsibilities, bond together, and love one another above all other human beings. People should marry with the understanding that they're entering into a very sacred bond or union. It is a permanent relationship that is not by blind chance. It is a very conscious choice.

Good marriages are based on commitment rather than feelings or sexual attraction.

The Importance of Romance in Marriage: Song of Songs 4:9–10[24]

Many couples have based their love on emotional feelings or sexual attraction, and when the honeymoon wears off, they feel they've made a mistake and wonder what has happened: the relationship feels dead.

God wants couples to continue on and on in their romantic love, but here's the deal: you have to work at it, just as you did when you were dating. Ladies, you used to put on your makeup, perfume your body, style your hair, say sweet things, make his favorite foods, laugh at his jokes, and enjoy his entertainment. These are the same things you must do after you've been married for a while. Likewise, guys, remember back to when you took a shower after work, changed clothes, put on cologne, asked her what she wanted to eat, took her out to dinner, and watched her favorite movie—just because you enjoyed being in her company. You took time just to be with her.

Let's read Song of Songs 4:9–10.[25] "You have stolen my heart, my sister, my bride; you have stolen my heart with one glance of your eyes, with one jewel of your necklace. How delightful is your love, my sister, my bride. How much more pleasing is your love than wine and the fragrance of your perfume than any spice."

Is that romantic, or what? God is giving married couples an idea of what to say to each other. The Song of Songs offers instruction (at least implicitly) on human behavior as it relates to sexuality and marriage. God is *not* a killjoy! He wants married couples to enjoy each other. God is the one who created sex and the pleasures that are derived from it.

Unfortunately, due to this act becoming perverted, many are unable to enjoy the benefits of married life. But there is hope. We'll explain more on this topic later.

Advice to Married Christians

"Let the husband render unto the wife due benevolence; and likewise also the wife unto the husband. The wife hath not power of her own body, but the husband; and likewise also the husband hath not power of his own body, but the wife. Defraud ye not one the other, except it be with consent for a time, that ye may give yourselves to fasting and prayer: and come together again, that Satan tempt you not for your incontinency" (1 Corinthians 7:35).

Not every man or woman is required to be married, but those who choose to be are permitted by Christianity to get married. The gospel does not interpose any hindrance to marriage and the normal creative relationship.

The word *benevolence* in Greek is *eumoia*, meaning "good will, kindness," and it is only found here and in Ephesians 6:7. It means that the wife and husband must respect each other regarding lawful sexual needs, pay the matrimonial debt, and render their conjugal duty to each other, mutually satisfying each other. If they do not obey this injunction, one may be responsible for the infidelity of the other.

The husband and wife belong to each other. Neither of them has any authority to refuse what the other needs—barring times of illness. All acts of perversion or unnatural affection must absolutely be rejected.

What you thus owe to each other, do not refuse to pay, unless it is by mutual consent for a time agreed upon for fasting and prayer. Then, regardless of the spiritual blessing either one has received, come together again to defeat Satan.

Marriage Holds Times of Great Joy

The Bible says that marriage holds times of great joy (Jeremiah 33:10–11[26]).

> Thus saith the Lord; Again there shall be heard in this place, which ye say shall be desolate without man and without beast, even in the cities of Judah, and in the streets of Jerusalem, that are desolate, without man, and without inhabitant and without beast. The voice of joy, and the voice of gladness, the voice of the bridegroom, and the voice of the bride, the voice of them that shall say, Praise the Lord of hosts; for the Lord is good; for his mercy endureth forever; and of them that shall bring the sacrifice of praise into the house of the Lord. For I will cause to return the captivity of the land, as at the first, saith the Lord.

God is able to bring great joy into the marriage union. But Jesus said in Revelation 3:20,[27] "Behold I stand at the door and knock." Jesus won't break down our doors. We must invite God into our marriages. When God is at the center of our homes, marriage can be fun, relaxing, happy, and joyful. Our moods are communicated through our voices. You can hear sorrow, despondency, victory, joy, and gladness within the voice.

There are times of great joy ahead for those whose hope is in the Lord. They will say, "Praise the Lord, for his mercy endures forever." Whenever we celebrate and laugh together, making Christ the center of our homes, there will be great joy!

Marriage Creates the Best Environment for Raising Children

Malachi 2:14–15[28] says, "Yet ye say, Wherefore? Because the Lord hath been witness between thee and the wife of thy youth, against whom thou hast dealt treacherously: yet is she thy companion, and the wife of thy covenant. And did not he make one? Yet had he the residue of the spirit. And wherefore one? That he might seek a godly seed. Therefore take heed to your spirit, and let none deal treacherously against the wife of his youth."

Perhaps you ask why. It is because the Lord is acting as the witness between you and the wife of your youth, because you have broken faith with her, though she is your partner, the wife of your marriage covenant. Has not the Lord made you one? In flesh and spirit, they are his. And why *one*? Because he seeks godly offspring. So guard yourself in your spirit, and do not break faith with the wife of your youth.

The following are statistics by Barbara Dafeo Whitehead on rethinking our commitment on marriage and family.

Children Suffer Most from the Breakdown of Marriage

The failure to protect our most vulnerable citizens—children—is a national crisis. Over one million children are affected by divorce each year. One third of all children are now born to unmarried mothers. The proportion of children growing up in single-parent families has now tripled in the last forty years. The lifetime negative consequences are now well-documented.

- **Crime**—Children not living in intact, married households have far higher rates of delinquency, youth crime, and alcohol and drug use. Those from father-absent families are twice as likely to be in jail as those from two-parent families.

• **Poverty**—Children living with a single mother are six times more likely to live in poverty as those who live with two biological parents.

• **Education**—Children not living with both parents are about twice as likely to drop out of high school and to have behavioral or psychological problems, while children of married parents tend to be more academically successful and emotionally stable.

• **Sex**—Adolescents not living with their biological parents are more likely to have out-of-wedlock sexual intercourse, followed by pregnancy and single parenthood. Today, one of every four American girls, aged fourteen to nineteen, is infected with a sexually transmitted disease![29]

The Divorce Culture: Rethinking Our Commitment to Marriage and Family

Studies conducted on the outcomes of children raised by single-parent families show, on average, that the economic and social well-being of children reared by a single parent is lower than that of children being raised in two-parent households. To many, these findings would seem self-evident. It is simply harder for one person to do the same work that two people working together are able to do.

The poverty rate for children living in single-parent homes is five times greater than for children living in two-parent homes. That fact has focused the political debate surrounding welfare reform squarely on the subject of marriage. In 1996, after many false starts, the Personal Responsibilities Work Opportunities, the Reconciliation Act (PRWORA) was signed into law. Under this law, the focus of welfare shifted from cash assistance for women and their children to an emphasis on self-sufficiency through work and enhanced financial support and involvement by fathers. One clearly stated intention of this legislation is to reduce out-of-wedlock births and to encourage the formation of two-parent families.

Some argue that the solution to poor, single-mother households is to go after the fathers and make them pay. Others say that preventing out-of-wedlock births in the first place, especially those involving teenage mothers, is a far better course of action, particularly since immature, unprepared, and uneducated teenagers tend to make poor parents—whether they are married or not.[30]

It is this author's opinion that an abortion is *not* a viable option for unwed mothers, but rather adoption or other arrangements that will benefit the child and its mother. God is able and willing to grant mercy, wisdom, and provision, even in the case of an unplanned pregnancy. God is the author of life and holds a high value on all human life.

The Importance of Fathers in Children's Asset Development

You may have heard this saying: "The greatest thing a man can do for his children is to love their mother." There is a lot of truth to that! Studies have shown for many years that the quality of the parents' relationship is predictive of their children's future marital success. But loving his children's mother is not the only important gift a father can give to his children. New studies are showing that fathers' involvement in their children's lives is strongly related to children's lifelong well-being.

The benefits of a father's involvement with his children begin during infancy. Despite traditional expectations, studies show that fathers can be as sensitive and responsive to their infant children as mothers. And a father's sensitivity can be very important. Infants whose fathers were closely involved with their care were found to be more cognitively developed at one year of age than infants with less-involved fathers. In addition, fathers' positive sensitive attitudes toward their infants were related to children's problem-solving competence later in life.

The importance of fathers' roles in their children's upbringing is also seen in the early and middle childhood years. Fathers' personality traits have been strongly related to their children's well-being. Children who were disliked by their peers commonly reported having poor relationships with their fathers.

Researchers have also found that women and men who get along well at work and in their personal relationships were likely to have had warm, loving relationships with competent, strong, and emotionally secure fathers who helped to nurture them while they were young.

Dads and Teens

During the adolescent years, fathers' attentiveness to their children was strongly related to their children's school achievement. A study of over thirty thousand high school seniors reported that 85 percent of "A" students had fathers who kept close track of how their children were doing in school.

Adolescents' relationship ties with fathers may be even more important when parents divorce and children live with their mothers—and this is especially important for boys. Both girls and boys have an easier time adjusting to their parents' divorce when conflict is low and the noncustodial parent (who is typically the father) maintains reliable and frequent contact with the children. Fathers who maintain involvement with their children—including participation in child rearing decisions and having some control over their children's upbringing—feel more comfort and closeness with their children and are more likely to make regular child support payments.

Perhaps more important, however, is the fact that resilient children who are able to bounce back from traumas or serious problems in their lives tend to come from families in which members have strong positive relationships with one another and who are emotionally supported by both parents.

The good news is that fathers are becoming more involved in their children's lives. Contrary to stereotypical beliefs about fathers and children, studies have found that nearly as many working men (72 percent) as working women (83 percent) felt conflict between their work and family responsibilities. Similarly, research indicates that men's family roles are just as important to them as their career roles, and fathers are reporting more frequently than in the past that involvement with their children and families is a source of personal satisfaction.

Clearly the father's involvement is important to children's intellectual and emotional development. We need to celebrate the contributions the father's make to the lives of their children.[31]

Unfaithfulness Breaks the Bond of Trust, the Foundation of All Relationships

Matthew 5:32[32] says, "But I tell you that anyone who divorces his wife, except for marital unfaithfulness, causes her to become an adulteress, and anyone who marries the divorced woman commits adultery."

Divorce today is just as pervasive as it was in Jesus' day. When either partner chooses to become unfaithful through the act of adultery or fornication, it is like taking a beautiful vase and breaking it. The bond of marital trust is broken, and families are devastated. This does not mean that divorce should automatically occur when a spouse commits adultery. Unfaithfulness implies a sexually immoral lifestyle, not a confessed and repented act of adultery. Forgiveness and reconciliation whenever possible is in keeping with God's heart. However, one should always remember that sin leads to death and separation. When trust is broken, it must be earned again through faithfulness and accountability.

In our culture today, the value of keeping one's oath or promise is taken carelessly and casually. Jesus emphasized the importance of telling the truth. It is better to keep an oath than to break it. Keeping our oaths and promises in marriage builds trust and is what makes committed human relationships possible. The Bible condemns making vows or taking oaths casually, especially when you know you won't keep it. Marriage is for covenant keepers who will be mature, forsaking all others and keeping their vows.

Marriage Is Permanent

Matthew 19:6[33] says, "So they are no longer two, but one. Therefore what God has joined together, let man not separate."

Some Pharisees came to Jesus to test him. They asked, "Is it lawful for a man to divorce his wife for any and every reason?"

"Haven't you read," he replied, "that at the beginning the creator made them male and female and said, 'For this reason a man will leave his father and mother, and be united to his wife, and the two will become one flesh'?"

The Pharisees hoped to trap Jesus. They were trying to trick Jesus by having him choose sides in a theological controversy. Two schools of thought represented two opposing views of divorce. One group supported divorce for almost any reason. The other believed that divorce could be allowed only for marital unfaithfulness. This conflict hinged on how each group interpreted Deuteronomy 24:1–4. In his answer, however, Jesus focused on marriage rather than divorce. He pointed out that God intended marriage to be permanent.

The divorce law is found in Deuteronomy 24:1–4.[34] In Moses' day, as well as in Jesus' day, the practice of marriage fell far short of God's intention. The same is true today. Jesus said that Moses gave this law only because of the people's hard hearts. Permanent marriage was God's intention, but because sinful human nature made divorce inevitable, Moses instituted some laws to help its victims. These were civil laws designed especially to protect the women who, in that culture, were quite vulnerable when living alone.

Because of Moses' law, a man could no longer just throw his wife out; he had to write a formal letter of dismissal. This was a radical step toward civil rights, for it made men think twice about divorce. God designed marriage to be indissoluble. Instead of looking for reasons to leave each other, God wants married couples to concentrate on how to stay together.

Moses' law says,

> When a man hath taken a wife, and married her, and it comes to pass that she finds no favour in his eyes, because he hath found some uncleanness in her; then let him write her a bill of divorcement, and give it in her hand, and send her out of his house. And when she is departed out of his house, she may go and be another man's wife. And if the latter husband hate her, and write her a bill of divorcement, and giveth it in her hand, and sendeth her out of his house; or if the latter husband die, which took her to be his wife; her former husband, which sent her away, may not take her again to be his wife, after that she is defiled; for that is an abomination before the Lord: and thou shalt not cause the land to sin, which the Lord thy God giveth thee for an inheritance. (Deuteronomy 24:1–4)

Ideally, Only Death Should Dissolve Marriage

Romans 7:2–3[35] says, "By law a married woman is bound to her husband as long as he is alive, but if her husband dies, she is released from the law of marriage. So then, if she marries another man while her husband is still alive, she is called an adulteress. But if her husband dies, she is released from the law and is not an adulteress, even though she marries another man."

Ideally, only death should dissolve marriage. God intended that marriage would provide the security that men and women need to grow in spirit, soul, and body. God wants marriage to be the nurturing ground whereby stability and love thrive.

Why is it best to live with one individual for life?

God designed marriage as the optimal way to bring glory to himself. What most people don't realize is that God didn't make the world for man but for himself. Genesis 1:27[36] says, "So God created man in *His* own image, in the image of *God* he created him; male and female he created them" (emphasis mine). God's design was for one man, one wife, and one lifetime.

Living with one individual for a lifetime challenges us to depend on God. Too often we depend on the marriage partner to provide all of our emotional needs. We make "gods" out of mere human beings, placing too many of our needs on a spouse instead of looking to the eternal, all-loving, all-righteous God to meet our spiritual needs. Marriage to one person challenges us to live the way Jesus taught us to be. It causes us to see our own faults and to practice forgiveness, not just to seek an "out." Marriage is God's gift to us. It takes a lifetime to understand and process the different phases of life.

Finally, the reason God chose one man, one wife, and one lifetime is that monogamy (the practice or state of being married to only one person at a time) provides sexual purity. Monogamy is a deterrent to sexually transmitted diseases, promoting better health over a lifetime. When individuals engage in multiple sexual encounters, the very soul (mind, will, and emotions) are affected. The Scripture says in 1 Corinthians 6:18[37] to "flee fornication, every sin that a man doeth is without the body; but he that committeth fornication sinneth against his own body."

For this and many other reasons, only death, ideally, should dissolve marriage.

Marriage is Based on the Principle and Practice of Love, Not Feelings

Ephesians 5:21–33[38] reads,

> Submit to one another out of reverence for Christ. Wives, submit to your husbands as to the Lord. For the husband is the Head of the wife as Christ is the head of the church, his body, of which he is the Savior. Now as the church submits to Christ, so also wives should submit to their husbands in everything. Husbands, love your wives, just as Christ loved the church and gave himself up for her to make her holy, cleansing her by the washing with water through the Word, and to present her to himself as a radiant church, without stain or wrinkle or any other blemish, but holy and blameless. In the same way, husbands ought to love their wives as their own bodies. He who loves his wife, loves himself. After all, no one ever hated his own body, but he feeds and cares for it, just as Christ does the church, for we are members of his body. For this reason a man will leave his father and mother and be united to his wife, and the two will become one flesh. This is a profound mystery—but I am talking about Christ and the church. However, each one of you must love his wife as he loves himself, and the wife must respect her husband.

Submission has become a misunderstood concept. It does not mean becoming a doormat. If Christ (to whom every knee will one day bow) submitted to his Father's will, then we too, being followers of Christ, must submit to him and to each other (Philippians 2:10).[39]

When we submit to God, we become more willing to obey his commands to submit to others. In a marriage relationship, both husband and wife are called to submit. For the wife, this means willingly following her husband's leadership in Christ. For the husband, it means putting aside his own interests in order to care for his wife. Submission is rarely a problem in homes where both partners have a strong relationship with Christ and are concerned for the happiness of the other. This kind of mutual submission preserves order and harmony in the family, while it increases love and respect among family members.

According to the Bible, the man is the spiritual head of the family, and his wife should acknowledge his leadership. But real spiritual leadership involves service. Just as Christ served the disciples, even to the point of washing the disciples' feet, so the husband is to serve his wife. A wise and Christ-honoring husband will not take advantage of his leadership role, and a wise and Christ-honoring wife will not try to undermine her husband's leadership.

In verses 22–28, why did Paul tell wives to submit and husbands to love? It could be that Christian women, newly freed in Christ, found submission difficult. Perhaps Christian men, used to the Roman custom that gave unlimited power to the head of the family, were not used to treating their wives with respect and love. Of course, both husband and wife should submit to each other (5:21), just as both should love the other.

In Ephesians 5:25–30,[40] Paul devotes twice as many words to telling husbands to love their wives as he does to telling wives to submit to their husbands. How should a man love his wife?

- He should be willing to sacrifice everything for her.
- He should make her well-being of primary importance.
- He should care for her as he cares for his own body.

No wife needs to fear submitting to a man who treats her in this way.

In Ephesians 5:31–33, the union of husband and wife merges two persons in such a way that little can affect one without also affecting the other. Oneness in marriage does not mean losing your personality in the personality of the other. Instead, it means caring for your spouse as you care for yourself, learning to anticipate his or her needs. It means helping the other person to become all he or she can be. The book of Genesis tells of God's plan that husbands and wives should be one (Genesis 2:24).

The power of the Word of God is often underestimated in its ability to bring clarity and give guidance in marriage. God's Word brings a fresh newness into the life of the marriage. It can defeat the powers of darkness and drive back the enemy.

Marriage Is a Living Symbol of Christ and the Church

Ephesians 5:23, 32[41] says, "For the husband is the head of the wife as Christ is the head of the church, his body of which he is the Savior. This is a profound mystery, but I am talking about Christ and the church."

Wives are called upon to submit to the authority of their own husbands as they would to that of Christ, the Lord. The chief threat in submitting to another person is the fear of being manipulated or mistreated by that person. There is no such cause for fear with Christ; his submission is tender guidance, not raw authority.

Yet, while Paul certainly does not imply that all (or any) husbands measure up to Christ in this regard, neither does he excuse wives from such submission because of the imperfection of their husbands. Whatever the hindrances, he is constantly aiming at the implementation of the sin-freed family of God. The metaphor of marriage, which illustrates the relationship between Christ and the church, becomes a two-way road, reflecting back upon that very relationship of man and woman in marriage.

As the church follows the leadership of its Savior, so must the wife follow her husband in everything. The strident protests and extreme feminism, though justified in many ways, cannot change the simple intent of this instruction. Yet much of that protest would perhaps never have arisen if teachers of the church had not stopped there but had gone on to round out the circle of mutual responsibility by giving men their proper exhortation: Men must love their wives, regardless of a lack of submission, in the same way that Christ loved the church when he sacrificed himself for it. The way in which husbands submit to their wives is by dying to their own interests out of concern for the best interests of their mates.

Christ's purpose in his self-sacrifice of love was to set the church apart for himself, as the newly re-created family of God, made as clean and pure and radiant as he is himself. Cleansing and purification are bestowed by the Word of promise and ritually applied to the individual believer in the water of Christian baptism. Christ's purpose, in other words, is the welfare and blossoming to full potential of the people in the new family.

Similarly, a husband sacrifices his own interests for his wife's sake, not so that she will start to make some self-improvements but so that she may grow toward maturity. To love one's wife in this way is to love oneself, which is no less than caring for one's own body. For, in yet another metaphor, the care we give our own bodies, e.g., grooming and feeding them, illustrates Christ's care for the church, the members of which are of his own body.

The argument for mutual submission in the sphere of matrimony is capped in Ephesians 5:31 by a quotation from Genesis 2:24: "For this cause shall a man leave his father and mother, and shall be joined unto his wife, and they two shall be one flesh." These verses reinforce the essential unity of marriage that takes precedence even over the relationship of parent and child.

Paul applies this mysterious unity metaphorically to the relationship between Christ and the church. "Marriage should be honored by all, and the marriage bed kept pure, for God will judge the adulterer and all the sexually immoral" (Hebrews 13:4[42]).

Here you have a recommendation of God's ordinance of marriage, which is honorable in all, and ought to be esteemed by all, and not denied to those to whom God has not denied it. It is honorable, for God instituted it for man in paradise, knowing it was not good for him to be alone. He married and blessed the first couple, the first parents of mankind, to direct all to look unto God in that great concern and to marry in the Lord.

Christ honored marriage with his presence and first miracle. It is honorable as a means to prevent impurity and a defiled bed. But whoremongers and adulterers God will judge. God knows those who are guilty of such sins. No darkness can hide them from him.

Taking Responsibility for Each Other's Welfare

In the previous chapter we talked about mutual submission. We want to transition by discussing the importance of taking responsibility for each other's welfare.

Philippians 2:3–5, 8[43] says, "Do nothing out of selfish ambition or vain conceit, but in humility consider others better than yourselves. Each of you should look not only to your own interests, but also to the interest of others. Your attitude should be the same as that of Christ Jesus ... And being found in appearance as a man he humbled himself."

Someone once said that the way up is the way down, referring to humility. The highest example of humility is found in our perfect example, Jesus Christ. Christ voluntarily laid aside his divine rights and privileges out of love for his Father. Our Lord gave his life on the cross for our sins, so we wouldn't have to face eternal death.

Christ displayed no selfishness in claiming his right to deity, although he was fully God and fully man. Often people excuse selfishness, pride, and arrogance by claiming their rights. They think, *It doesn't matter if I'm late; I deserve to take my time getting ready*, or *I can spend all this money on myself; I worked hard for it*, or *I can get an abortion; I have a right to control my own body*.

But as believers, we should have a different attitude, one that enables us to lay aside our rights in order *to serve others*. If we say we follow Christ, we must also say that we want to live as he lived. We should develop his attitude of humility as we serve, even when our efforts are not acknowledged.

Since Christian marriage is God's model for success, let us discuss the practical needs of each gender and each role. What do husbands need? We would do well to memorize these needs.

Genesis 2:18[44] says, "The Lord God said, 'It is not good for the man to be alone. I will make a helper suitable for him.'"

Man needs help.

Interestingly, it was God who determined that it was not good for man to be alone (Genesis 2:18–25[45]). There is no indication that Adam himself was dissatisfied with his circumstances. After making his evaluation (v. 18a), God proposed a solution. He would provide a *helper* for Adam. God was already Adam's helper, but a *superior* one. The animals were also Adam's helpers, but *inferior* ones. This new helper, then, had to be one that would be equal to him. The Hebrew word for *suitable* suggests something that completes a polarity, as the North Pole is "suitable" to the South Pole. One without the other is incomplete.

God administered anesthesia to Adam, and while the man was in a deep sleep, God made woman from one of his ribs. The Hebrew word is *panah*, meaning "skillfully formed." Actually, the text says that the Lord "builded" woman.

When Adam said that the woman was "bone of my bones and flesh of my flesh," he was giving the ancient equivalent of our "in weakness and strength." One of the meanings of the verb behind the noun *bone* is "to be strong." *Flesh*, on the other hand, represents *weakness* in a person. Woman is said not to have been taken out of man's head to be lorded over by him, nor from his feet to be trampled on by him, but from his side to be equal with him, from under his arm to be protected by him, and from near his heart to be loved by him.

The man is to leave his father and mother (neither of which Adam had) and cleave to his wife. Elsewhere in the Old Testament, these are covenant terms. When Israel forsook God's covenant, she "left" him. And when Israel was obedient to God's covenant, she "cleaved" to him. Genesis 2:24 is saying that marriage is a covenant, simply through the use of covenant terminology.

The climax of creation was this: the man and his wife were both naked. How appropriate! This verse claims a total transparency between this primal couple, a man needs the tender love of his wife.

The Wife's Responsibilities to the Husband

Some key passages are found in Scripture: Genesis 2:18–25;[46] Proverbs 31:10–31;[47] Ephesians 5:22–24, 33;[48] Titus 2:4–5;[49] 1 Peter 3:1–6.[50] The idea of submission makes porcupine quills pop out of many women. Sometimes this is because she believes that she may be mistreated. Many false pictures arise from the subject of submission. Let's discuss what submission is *not*.

1. Submission is not just a concept for women. It is a concept for all believers. (Compare Ephesians 5:21;[51] Philippians 2:3–4;[52] 1 Peter 5:5;[53] and Hebrews 13:17.[54])

2. Submission does not mean that the wife takes on the role of a slave. Actually the wife is free through submission to become all that God intended her to be. (See Proverbs 31:10–31.[55])

3. Submission does not mean that the wife never gives advice, has an opinion, or opens her mouth. (Compare Proverbs 31:26;[56] Acts 18:26;[57] and Judges 13:21–23.[58])

4. Submission does not mean that the wife becomes a wallflower who allows her capabilities to become dormant.

5. Submission does not mean that the wife is inferior to the husband. Jesus Christ was not inferior to Mary and Joseph, and yet the Bible says that as a child he became subject to them (Luke 2:51[59]). Jesus was in no way inferior to God the Father. He was and is completely and fully God in every sense, yet the Scriptures assert that there is order and structure within the Trinity. Jesus said, "I do not seek my own will, but the will of him who sent me" (John 5:30[60]).

In the same way, the submission of the wife in no way implies inferiority. Instead, it teaches the necessity for order and structure within the home.

Having shown what submission is not, let's look at what it *is*.

1. Scripture indicates that the wife's responsibility is to make herself submissive. *Nowhere is the husband told to force his wife physically into submission.*
2. The wife's submission is to be a continuous lifestyle.
3. Wifely submission is mandatory, not optional. The Greek verb is in the imperative mood. Her submission is not based upon the way her husband treats her. Nor is it based upon the husband's abilities, talents, wisdom, education, or spiritual state.
4. Submission is a spiritual matter. It is to be done "as to the Lord" (Ephesians 5:22).[61] The Lord commands the wife to be submissive. Refusal to submit to the husband is therefore rebellion against God himself. Submission to the husband is a test of her love for God as well as a test of love for her husband. Further, submission is a spiritual matter, because it must be performed in the power of the Holy Spirit by women who are being strengthened in the inner man by the Holy Spirit and who are being filled up to all the fullness of God. (Compare Ephesians 1:1–5:21; 1 Peter 1:1–3:6.)
5. Submission is not a negative but a *positive* concept. Submission means that the wife uses all of her abilities under the management of her husband for the good of her husband and family. Submission means she sees herself as part of her husband's team. She is not her husband's opponent, fighting at cross-purposes or trying to outdo him. She is not merely an individual going her separate way. She is on her husband's team, striving for the same goal. She has opinions, ideas, desires, requests, and insights, and she lovingly makes them known. But she knows that on any good team, someone has to

make the final decisions. She knows that the team members must support the team leader or no progress will be made, and confusion and frustration will result.

6. The wife is to submit with a respectful attitude. Submission is to be the wife's *lifestyle at all times, in all places, and in everything.*

Now, before you thoroughly gag, know that this certainly does *not* mean that she must obey her husband when he asks her to do what God forbids or tries to keep her from doing what God commands. She is to be subject to her husband "as is fitting in the Lord." Since the husband's authority is delegated to him, he loses his authority at these times and in those areas when his directives are clearly contrary to the revealed will of God as it is found in Scripture. When the husband asks her to do that which is unmistakably contrary to the Word of God, the wife must obey God rather than man (Acts 5:28–29).[62]

The wife's submission to her husband, then, is to be extensive but not necessarily total or unlimited. She is to obey him in everything except that which contradicts the Word of God. This would include watching pornography via movies or the Internet and engaging in illegal or immoral activities. She may explain her position firmly, calmly, and lovingly.

An honest examination of Scripture leads us to the conclusion that *the wife's primary ministry in life is to her husband.*

In Genesis 2:18–22[63] there are several important facts that emerge.

1. God made the woman to be man's helper. Without the woman, man, even in his perfect condition, was incomplete.

2. God made the woman to be a suitable helper. None of the animals could provide the kind of help that man needed. Only woman could do that.

3. God created the woman to correlate with the man. She is man's compliment, not an exact duplicate. She gives him *comfort and courage.*

According to Scripture, the wife was made to fill the needs, lacks, and inadequacies of her husband. She was made to be her husband's unique helper. Proverbs 31:12[64] says she will do him good and not evil all the days of her life.

Morally, the husband should be able to trust her around his friends, knowing that she will be loyal and faithful to him.

She should be able to be trusted with money, not over-extending the credit cards or pressuring the husband to live beyond their means.

I would like to specifically suggest some ways she may be helpful to her husband.

1. Maintaining a daily devotional life (1 Peter 3:1–2, 7).[65]
2. Keeping herself beautiful, especially in the inner person (1 Peter 3:3–5).[66]
3. Maintaining a "Christ-like" attitude (Philippians 4:4).[67]
4. Making the home an emotionally safe place, being careful not to make belittling remarks.
5. Being trustworthy and dependable (Proverbs 31:11–12).[68]
6. Endeavoring to discuss things openly, honestly, and lovingly (Ephesians 4:25).[69]
7. Showing an interest in his problems and concerns (Philippians 2:3–4).[70]
8. Being longsuffering, forgiving, and forbearing (Ephesians 4:2, 31–32).[71]
9. Being content with her possessions and her tasks (Hebrews 13:5, 16).[72]

10. Being ambitious and diligent, contributing to the team of her marriage (Psalm 128:3;[73] Proverbs 31:10–31[74]).
11. Building a united front in guiding the children. Children pick up on the attitudes of the mother. If she shows disrespect, the children will also. All differences of opinions should be settled away from the children, speaking in a way that brings Christ glory.
12. Being grateful to him. Appreciation should be expressed freely and in many different ways.
13. Showing confidence in his ability to make decisions. Lack of confidence, disdain, anxiety, and strong opposition over his decisions may cause him to be reactionary, defensive, or indecisive. She should ask questions in a nonthreatening way.

If you have felt convicted by the spirit of God because you're not the wife God wants you to be, remember that there is hope through repentance by turning from your sin. The following steps will help you.

- Admit your sin to God and to your husband.
- Seek cleansing from your sins through the blood of Christ (Ephesians 1:7;[75] 1 John 1:9[76]).
- Ask the Holy Spirit for power to change (Galatians 5:16, 22–23).[77]
- Move out in obedience to the Scriptures, and make the necessary changes (Philippians 2:12–13).[78]

Wives or potential wives, I've tried to lay a biblical foundation for our responsibilities in the marriage union. Now, let's begin looking at the husband's role. Compared to the husband's responsibilities, our role is much simpler. Husbands are the ones who will answer to God for the stewardship of their families. Proceeding forward, what is the role of the husband?

The Husband's Responsibilities to the Wife

The husband's main responsibility is to provide loving leadership (Ephesians 5:22).[79] This may be highlighted by asking two questions: Husbands, do you love your wives enough to die for them? Wives, do you love your husbands enough to live for them?

Ephesians 5:25–33[80] explains the meaning of the husband's leadership and obligations.

> Husbands, love your wives just as Christ also loved the church and gave himself up for her that he might sanctify her, having cleansed her by the washing of water with the Word, that he might present to himself the church in all her glory, having no spot or wrinkle or any such stain, that she should be holy and blameless, so husbands ought also to love their wives as their own bodies. He who loves his own wife, loves himself, for no one ever hated his own flesh but nourished and cherishes it, just as Christ also does the church. Because we are members of his body, for this cause a man should leave his father and his mother and cleave to his wife and the two shall become one flesh. This mystery is great, but I am speaking with reference to Christ and the church; nevertheless, let each individual among you also love his own wife even as himself and let the wife see to it that she respects her husband. (Ephesians 5:25–33)[81]

Compared to Paul's words to the husbands, wives have it relatively simple; they are to submit. Submission to one another rubs us the wrong way, because we don't like to submit, and the "old man" rebels within. Yet compared to what Jesus Christ requires for husbands, Christian wives have an easy responsibility.

Let's look at the responsibility God has placed on the husband. As a follower of Christ, he is responsible to lead his family. God has placed him as the head of his home. Headship means leadership. It doesn't just mean rights and privileges. It does not mean merely wearing the uniform and having the right to give the final word. It also means assuming the responsibilities that go with such authority.

Please read these key passages in the Bible that speak of the man's part in marriage: Genesis 3:16;[82] Ephesians 5:23–33;[83] 1 Timothy 3:4–5;[84] Psalm 128;[85] 1 Peter 3:7;[86] 1 Corinthians 7:3–4;[87] Proverbs 5:15–19;[88] Colossians 3:19.[89] These passages reflect two primary responsibilities of the husband toward his wife:

- He is to be his wife's leader.
- He is to be his wife's lover.

The Husband as His Wife's Leader

According to Ephesians 5:23;[90] 1 Timothy 3:4–5, 12;[91] and 1 Corinthians 11:3;[92] the husband is to be his wife's leader.

In our current times, we think of the leader as someone in a role, cranking out orders. But this is contrary to biblical leadership.

Matthew 20:20–28[93] gives us God's concept of a leader. According to this passage, a leader is first and foremost a servant. His concern is not for himself; his concern is not to give orders, to boss other people around, or to have his own way. His concern is to meet the needs of others. Indeed, if the best interests of others are not on his heart—if he is not willing to sacrifice himself, his personal needs, wants, desires, aspirations, time, and money, and if the needs of others are not more important than his own—he is not qualified to lead.

John 13:1–15[94] gives us the same picture of what it means to be a leader. In this passage, the emblems of leadership are not a throne or a club but a towel and a basin. In other words, a leader must have a servant's heart. And if he has a servant's heart, he will reflect the heart of Christ.

When we apply this biblical concept of leadership to the husband, we see that being the leader means that he must be the family's *biggest servant*.

Jesus Christ is our model of the perfect servant leader. In Philippians 2:6–8,[95] Paul's letter to the Philippians says this about Jesus: "Who being in the form of God thought it not robbery to be equal with God; but made himself of no reputation, and took upon him the form of a servant, and was made in the likeness of man: and being found in fashion as a man. He humbled himself, and became obedient unto death, even the death of the cross."

Just as Christ ransomed himself for all humanity, he charges husbands with loving their wives as Christ loved the church and gave himself for it (Ephesians 5:23–33).[96]

The way that Jesus Christ led his disciples for over a three-year period is an excellent model to follow. Let's observe:

Jesus continually associated with his disciples, whom he led (John 1:39, 43;[97] Mark 1:17; 3:4, 10, 14; 5:1, 30–31, 40; 6:1).[98] He didn't send text messages, short e-mails, write a few letters, or visit infrequently. He didn't spend long hours away from them. He continually spent time with them, talking about the most important things of life (Matthew 5:2).[99]

In 1 Peter 3:7[100] Peter commands husbands to dwell or live with their wives. The husband who does not enjoy regular and frequent companionship with his wife is not fulfilling his God-given responsibility. Many husbands have not left their father and mother emotionally, and they cling to their families of origin for their emotional and social interaction. But God's original blueprint for marriage is designed for oneness. Unless there is intimacy/nakedness/transparency with the spouse, there can be no oneness. Jesus took the time to create fellowship and intimacy with his disciples, setting the example for husbands to follow.

If a husband wants to be followed, he must learn to follow the greatest teacher of all, Jesus Christ. Frequently we read in the gospels, "Follow me," or "Come after me," or "I have left you an example." He did not simply tell men, "You ought to pray"; he modeled being a man of prayer. The Scripture records in Mark 1:35[101]: "Rising while before day Jesus went out to pray." His life was a living example of how he wanted men to live in every aspect. The husband should strive to continually practice a pattern of godliness, holiness, dedication, compassion, and devotion to God.

Because we live in a fallen world and we struggle with the sinful nature, husbands will not always be the perfect examples. However, that should not be an excuse for not practicing godliness. The Bible says, "And if any man sin, we have an advocate with the Father, Jesus Christ the righteous" (1 John 2:1).[102] When a husband fails, he should be quick to admit his wrong to God and his wife, asking for forgiveness and then dealing with whatever the issue is.

Jesus Christ led his disciples by delegating responsibilities and making decisions. (Compare John 4:1–2;[103] Mark 1:35–39;[104] John 11:39–44;[105] Matthew 10:1–14.[106])

When Jesus delegated responsibility, he gave clear, concise, and specific directions so that the disciples knew how to go about their tasks.

Husbands are called upon to *lead*, which involves decision making and delegating responsibility. In a marriage relationship, there needs to be someone who has the final authority; otherwise chaos and confusion will result. Fifty-fifty marriages are impossible. They do not work. In marriage God has established the husband as the final decision maker. The wife is to be the husband's helper. She is to be his chief advisor, resource person, and consultant. If the wife's opinion differs from the husband's on major issues where there is no scriptural directive, the husband should be very careful about forcing his opinion upon the wife. They should pray about the matter, and if necessary, seek godly counsel before a final decision is made. On the other hand, God does not want the husband to be indecisive or fearful about making decisions and delegating responsibilities, nor must he relinquish his decision making and delegating responsibilities to his wife.

The wise husband will utilize his wife's gifts and talents. Some women are accountants. Some are mortgage brokers, insurance agents, doctors, teachers, or social workers. The wise husband will tap into his wife's skills and utilize her abilities, whether degreed or not. Her advice could save the family money or afford other blessings or opportunities.

The Husband as His Wife's Lover

Dr. Jay Adams, an author, counselor, and seminary professor, has combined the two concepts of leading and loving, saying that "in the home the husband is to provide loving leadership."

The wife has such a great *need* for love—and the husband sometimes has such a great *lack* of love—that God's command that the husband love his wife appears three times within the space of a few verses in Ephesians 5. Twice in this passage, God enjoins the husband to love his wife, even as he loves himself (vv. 28, 33). One time, God instructs the husband to love his wife just as Christ also loved the church (v. 25). Oceans of truth concerning the husband's relationships to his wife are opened to us by these verses.

Normally, a man uses a lot of time and gives a great deal of thought, effort, and money to take care of himself. His needs, desires, aspirations, hopes, and comfort are very important to him. He nourishes and cherishes himself. He carefully protects and provides for the needs of his body. He does not deliberately do that which would bring harm to himself. When he is hungry, he eats. When he is thirsty, he drinks. When he is tired, he sleeps. When he is in pain, he goes to the doctor. When he cuts himself, he washes the wound and binds it up. When he sees an object coming toward him, he put his hands up for protection. He naturally, carefully, and fervently nourishes and cherishes himself.

Well, the Scripture indicates, *this is the way a man is to love his wife. He is to nourish her, cherish her, protect her, satisfy her, provide for her, care for her, and sacrifice for her—to the same degree and extent, and in the same manner, as he does for himself.*

Now, that's a lot of love that a husband is to have for his wife. And although it is a high standard for a husband to keep, but there is still a higher one.

Scripture says, "Husbands, love your wives just as Christ also loved the church."

The love of Christ cannot be measured. Its dimensions are too high, too wide, and too deep to be able to comprehend fully. But this we know: that Jesus loved humanity so much that he gave his all for the church. So ought men to love their wives. Now that's the most profound love anyone could ever encounter.

What do we know about the love of Christ for his people?

- *It is an unconditional love.* Romans 5:8[107] says, "But God demonstrates his own love for us in this: while were still sinners, Christ died for us."
- *It is a free will love.* He chooses to love us. Ephesians 1:6–7[108] says, "To the praise of his glorious grace, which he has freely given us in the one he loves."
- *It is a deep love.* John 13:1b[109] says, "Having loved his own

who were in the world, he now showed them the full extend of his love."

- *It is an endless love.* Jeremiah 31:3b[110] says, "I have loved you with an everlasting love: I have drawn you with loving kindness." Romans 8:39 says, "Neither height, nor depth, nor anything else in all creation will be able to separate us from the love of God that is in Christ Jesus our Lord."
- *It is a selfless love.* Philippians 2:6–7[111] says, "Who being in the very nature of God, did not consider equality with God something to be grasped, but made himself nothing, taking the very nature of a servant being made in human likeness."
- *It is a meaningful love.* He wants our growth, our happiness, and our well-being. Ephesians 5:26–27[112] says, "To make her holy, cleansing her by the washing with water through the Word. And to present her to himself as a radiant church without stain or wrinkle or any other blemish, but holy and blameless."

Wayne A. Mack writes, "It is a sacrificial love. He loved us and gave himself for us. He died, the just for the unjust, to bring us to God. In love, He endured the horrible death of the cross with all of its physical and spiritual torture and agony. In love, He bore the guilt and penalty of sin and the wrath of God in the place of his people. In love, He personally bore our sins in His own body on the cross so that the penalty and power and devastating effects of sin in our lives might be broken" (Ephesians 5:2, 25;[113] Galatians 2:20;[114] 1 Peter 3:18;[115] Romans 5:6–11;[116] 1 Peter 2:24[117]).

It is a *manifested* love. Christ manifests his love in words and deeds. He tells us he loves us. He shows us he loves us. He protects us, prays for us, guards us, strengthens us, helps us, defends us, teaches us, comforts us, chastens us, equips us, empathizes with us, and provides for all our needs" (John 10:1–14;[118] 14:1–3;[119] 13:34–35;[120] 15:9–10;[121] Romans 8:32;[122] Philippians 4:13, 19;[123] Hebrews 4:14–16[124]).

This is the measuring rod by which a husband is to evaluate his relationship with his wife. It is important that husbands give honor to their wives as unto the weaker vessel. Otherwise the husband's prayers may be hindered (1 Peter 3:7[125]).

How can a husband communicate love to his wife? Here are a few ways:

1. One of the most neglected yet simplest ways is by saying, "I love you." *I love you* is like music to a woman's ears; it causes her to feel valued. Saying those words once at the altar on the wedding day is not enough. Wives have a great need to be loved and cherished.

2. A wife has varied needs. You may provide for the satisfaction of them. A wife has physical, emotional, intellectual, social, recreational, sexual, and spiritual needs. Those needs may come across like this: "Will you rub my feet? Support me as I teach? Quiz me on this test? I'd like to spend time with some friends. Let's go traveling abroad. Let's make love. Let's read the Bible together. I need to spend time in prayer." Remember that God wants you to be concerned about every area of her needs.

3. You may love her by protecting her (Ephesians 5:28[126]).
   - A wife needs physical protection. It is unwise and selfish to ask her to go alone to the store in the middle of the night to obtain something you could live without.
   - She may be doing more than she is physically capable of doing.
   - She may need your help with the demands of caring for children. This can take a toll on a woman's body.

- The criticism or expectations of others may be overwhelming to her. Stand up for her honor in the presence of family and others when necessary.

4. You may express your love by giving respect and courtesy, e.g., not talking on your cell phone when going out to dinner, and not making cutting remarks to or about her in front of other people.

   - Speak to her in a gentle tone instead of rough speech. Be a gentleman.

   - Treat her as a valuable jewel. Remember that she is part of you.

5. You may show your love by assisting her with chores and responsibilities. Many husbands think it is not masculine to wash dishes, care for the children, shop, or clean the house. Some husbands will tell the wife that the baby is crying, but will not get up to find out *why* the baby is crying, expecting all the physical care and nurturing to come from the mother. As I have shared earlier in this manual, fathers are vitally important to their infant children.

6. You may express your love by sacrificing for her. One woman shared a story of the rent being due. When she asked her husband for the money to pay the rent, he said, "Honey, I'm sorry, but I don't have it. You see, there's an expensive watch I've wanted to buy for myself, and I've been putting down money all along. If I don't pay for it now, I'll lose it." The wife then had to seek assistance to avoid eviction. Later on, the wife recounted that someone stole her husband's watch.

   Needless to say, God requires that the husband sacrifice for his wife, just as Christ did for the church. If a husband denies himself what he wants, he is saying *I love you* to her in a very loud and clear voice.

7. You may love your wife by allowing her to really share your life. Intimacy begins when there is true emotional sharing. When the husband begins to share his dreams, his hurts, his past, his hopes, and his future, he is letting his wife into his world. The wife begins to feel their oneness and can be supportive to him. This is the foundation of trust: to take a risk and become vulnerable.

8. You may express your love by refusing to compare her unfavorably to other women. The intention may be to challenge her to make some improvements, but it will instead create insecurity, jealousy, and resentment. This is an area not safe to travel in!

9. You may express your love by giving praise and appreciation in generous and large doses.

   • Never laugh at or belittle the small things she may do for you.

   • Express appreciation for her ideas, character, opinions, prayers, insight, cooking, cleaning, and satisfying your physical needs. Do your very best to make your wife feel she is the most appreciated and loved women in the world.

Husbands, you are to be your wife's leader and lover this is a responsibility only you can uniquely fulfill. *Putting these facts into practice* will promote oneness. If you have noted areas where failure has occurred:

• Admit your sin to God and your wife (1 John 1:9;[127] Matthew 5:23–24;[128] James 5:16[129]).

• Seek cleansing from this sin—through the blood of Jesus Christ (Ephesians 1:7).[130]

- Ask God's Holy Spirit for the power to change (Luke 11:13;[131] Galatians 5:16, 22–23[132]).
- Move out in obedience to the Word of God and make necessary changes (Philippians 2:12–13;[133] James 1:19–24[134]).

Twenty Commands Concerning Marriage: 1 Corinthians 7:10–39

1. Let every man have his own wife (v. 2).
2. Let every woman have her own husband.
3. Let the husband meet the sexual needs of the wife (vv. 3–4).
4. Let the wife meet the sexual needs of her husband (vv. 3–4).
5. Defraud not each other in sexual matters; pay your conjugal vows.
6. Come together again after you have consented to live continent for a period so as to pray and fast (v. 5).
7. Let both men and women marry if they have battles of self-control (v. 9).
8. Let not the wife depart from her husband (v. 10).
9. If she does depart, let her remain unmarried or be reconciled to her husband (v. 11).
10. Let not the husband divorce his wife (v. 11).
11. Let not the Christian man divorce the non-Christian if she be pleased to dwell with him. The reason is in verses 12–16.
12. Let not the Christian wife divorce her husband if he be pleased to dwell with her (vv. 13–16).
13. If the unbeliever departs and refuses to live with the Christian, let him depart. Do not force continuance of the marriage. The Christian is freed from the marriage bonds in such cases (v. 15).
14. Let every man or woman remain as he or she was when each became a Christian (vv. 17–24). That is, do not use Christianity as an excuse to break up your own home and perhaps another, seeking a new companion.
15. If you are bound to a wife, seek not to be loosed. Stay in the same calling and state in which your were saved (vv. 17–24).

16. If you are loosed from a wife, seek not another wife (v. 27). If you do marry, however, you have not sinned (v. 28).
17. You that have wives, live as though you did not have them (v. 29–31)—that is, free from anxiety (vv. 32–35).
18. Let the father who has a daughter of marriageable age be free to give her in marriage. It is no sin for him to do so or for the virgin to marry (vv. 36–38).
19. The wife is bound by law to be married as long as the husband lives (v. 39). Marriage is for the lifetime of the spouse.
20. Christians must remarry only Christians when companions die or divorce occurs. (v. 39)

Seven Reasons Marriage Is Indissoluble: Matthew 19:9

1. Marriage was *divinely* instituted in the beginning. God made them male and female (vv. 4, 6, 8).

2. God gave an expressed commandment that the man leave his father and mother and cleave or be bonded to his wife and they both shall be one flesh. Let no man put asunder or separate them (vv. 5–6).

3. Adam and Eve did not divorce each other (v. 8).

4. Marriage makes a man and woman one in flesh, with complete union of goals, finances, hopes, joys, sorrows, and being companions for life (vv. 5–6).

5. Divorce can bring harmful consequences to both partners, to their children, and to others, and they may entangle themselves with sin (v. 9; Mark 7:21; Romans 1:29–32).

6. Along with divorce come other temptations of evil (v. 9; Galatians 5:19–21).

7. There is no excuse under the gospel for "hardness of heart" against each other (2 Corinthians 5:17–18; Ephesians 4:24; Galatians 5:24).

The New Testament gives *exceptions* to this law:

1. Fornication (Matthew 5:32; 19:9)

2. Willful desertion because of Christ and the gospel (1 Corinthians 7:12–15)

3. Death (Romans 7:2)

4. Adultery (Matthew 5:32)

Serious Road Blocks In Marriages

As we have discovered in previous chapters, God's original blueprint for marriage is *oneness*—spiritually, mentally, emotionally, physically, and socially. Marriage is a *covenant commitment for life* that both partners must be willing to be faithful to.

Unfortunately, due to sin and its devastating effects on humanity, this, in some cases, is not possible. Therefore, God in his divine wisdom outlined a scriptural basis on which separation, divorce, and remarriage may take place. In the next pages, we will discover these reasons for which divorce and remarriage are permitted.

There are four conditions under which one may *remarry*: death, adultery, fornication, and desertion. Likewise, there are five conditions under which one may be *separated*: the aforementioned reasons along with the inability to dwell together peacefully. However, in this last situation, one may not divorce.

When two professing believers cannot get along in marriage, what might some of the causes be?

Unmet Expectations

Oftentimes when couples marry without getting to know each other well, they enter into the marriage with assumptions. For example, a woman who observed her father as the cook in the family may believe that it is her husband's role to cook. The man, in turn, may assume that, because he saw his mother getting up for work early every morning, his wife also will not mind working outside of the home.

In both of the aforementioned scenarios, one partner assumed that the couple would assume roles that their parents had viewed as appropriate. Problems transpire when expectations are not met and the picture of marriage that each had in mind is not the reality of their relationship.

The Level of Spirituality within the Marriage

Although they may both profess Christianity, the couple may share different views on the spiritual disciplines. One of the partners may not feel it is important to pray together, read the Bible, or have daily family devotions, while the other may feel it is of the utmost importance. One partner may not agree with the particular theological views of the partner's church, opting to attend a different fellowship.

Each should understand that Christ is the threefold cord that can hold a marriage together. Christ in the center of the relationship is what gives the marriage the strength to weather life's storms. A conscientious commitment to pray together as a couple invites the "author" of marriage into the home.

Money Disagreements

Who will manage the money? Who will have the most discipline and manage it wisely? What are the spending habits?

When couples cannot or will not answer the money questions, they are creating a big rift in the relationship that may cause major problems. Without accountability of how purchases will be made and how much will be spent, emotional separation will occur with an attitude that says, *This is my money, and I won't let you tell me how to spend it.* Other questions will arise: Should they have joint or separate accounts? Will they tithe and give offerings?

These are questions with answers, but unless both husband and wife are willing to seek the answers together, money may cause division.

Christian believers are able to overcome this area by reaching out to a pastor or a trustworthy financial counselor with biblical views.

The Word of God declares, "A house divided against itself cannot stand." If the married couple made a covenant relationship before God, it is imperative that they both seek help immediately in this area.

Poor Communication

When the husband and wife speak to one another in unkind words or tones, it erodes the relationship. Poor communication can be shown in verbal or nonverbal ways, such as not giving the other person eye contact, texting someone else while the partner is speaking to them, or talking on the cell phone while out to dinner with the spouse. These behaviors say, *You do not have my full attention, and what you're saying is unimportant.*

Failure to communicate plans without the input of the other spouse shows a lack of respect. Demeaning the spouse publicly by calling the person names or saying, e.g., "John doesn't know what he's talking about. Let me tell you what really happened." Poor communication can destroy a marriage, because communication is the lifeblood of any relationship—and particularly marriage. Without healthy, loving communication, the marriage may not thrive.

Healthy communication is possible. It is an art that can be acquired. The first step is to choose kindness. Jesus modeled kindness, which is love in action. The Scripture says to let your conversation be always full of grace, seasoned with salt, so that you may know how to answer everyone (Colossians 4:6).[135] James 3:1–11 gives wonderful instruction on the power of the tongue.

Sexual Intimacy

In the sharing one's body in the act of sexual intercourse, a deep sense of oneness, unity, and love may be expressed. God created sex to be a wonderful source of fulfillment between the husband and wife (1 Corinthians 7:2–5).[136]

- Problems may occur if one of the mates wants to engage more often than the other or is inconsiderate of the others feelings.
- Problems may occur if there is a significant age difference and physical health issues prohibit its frequency.
- Problems of satisfaction may occur when either partner compares the spouse to a previous relationship.
- Problems may occur if one partner senses that he or she really doesn't matter to the other and that his or her body is being used to satisfy a spouse with selfish motives.
- Problems may occur if both spouses experienced sexual abuse, and has not received proper counseling.
- Problems may occur if a spouse does not practice cleanliness, causing hygiene odors.

It is important that the marriage bed be sanctified and holy, meaning that you are to give your love fully and completely to your spouse, "Forsaking all others."

With appropriate counsel, sexual problems can be overcome. God is the author and creator of sex. It is his will that the husband and wife enjoy each other fully!

The Inability to Forgive and Move Forward

Billy Graham once said, "Marriage is made up of two great forgivers."

The ability to forgive offenses and to move forward is a choice that a follower of Jesus Christ can choose to make. There's an old saying that says, "To err is human; to forgive is divine." Jesus said that if we don't forgive others, God will not forgive us.

When spouses hold on to resentments and past hurtful memories, bitterness develops within the marriage, causing erosion, and little by little the life of the marriage suffers.

If the nature of the offense was not adultery or fornication (which does not have to lead to divorce if true repentance is evident), the offended mate needs to seek God on their knees in prayer, asking God to help them let the offense go and not bring it up again. It may take much prayer, but it is better to humble oneself before God in prayer than to throw away a relationship and family that could be salvaged. Ask Jesus to grant a heart of tenderness. The power of the Holy Spirit will enable the offended mate to forgive, and the hardness of heart will eventually soften. With God, all things are possible.

Adultery Allows for Remarriage

Paul and Ruth

Ruth and Paul met in Seattle, Washington, during a youth revival. She was eighteen, and he was twenty-one. They married and decided to move back to Paul's home state of Michigan.

Paul had come from a two-parent family of seven siblings. Ruth had come from a broken home but had known the care of a loving father. Early in their marriage, there were reports of sexual immorality, but Ruth did not want to believe them, especially since she and Paul had three children, each one year apart. A young woman of the church reported that Paul, being a youth pastor, had sexually violated her.

This accusation went as far as a court hearing. Ruth appeared with her husband in court in support of him. Ruth's mother-in-law said that the family must stay together, no matter what. Paul was acquitted of any wrongdoing.

As the years went on, there were other allegations of Paul being seen soliciting prostitutes. Each time Ruth confronted Paul, he denied any wrongdoing, though in Ruth's mind, she suspected immorality.

Paul, however, was a good provider, and had educated himself over the years, receiving his bachelor's degree while still upholding a position as an associate pastor. Paul's job allowed him to travel across country.

Ruth discovered the reality that Paul was committing adultery. She asked for marriage counseling, and he consented. Off and on, for several years, they both attended counseling.

After one of Paul's business trips, a woman began to call their home, saying that she was pregnant and Paul was the father. When Ruth didn't give the desired response, the woman began relentlessly calling the church where Paul and Ruth attended, saying that she was pregnant and Paul was the father.

The pastor of the church confronted Paul with the accusation. Paul sheepishly owned up to his adulterous behavior. After twenty years and no repentance on Paul's part, Ruth filed for divorce on the biblical grounds of adultery.

Old and New Testament Discussion on Divorce

Matthew 5:31–32[137] says, "Whoever divorces his wife, let him give her a divorce certificate. But I say to you, whoever divorces his wife except on the grounds of [her] infidelity exposes her to adultery, and whoever marries a divorced woman involves himself in adultery."

Here, then, are the two contrasting positions.

The first was discussed and debated by the scribes and Pharisees, based on opinions expressed by the men of long ago, and amounted to this: when a wife was to be dismissed, a certificate of divorce had to be properly drawn up and given to her.

The second position was held by Jesus. He asked the question, *Why divorce at all?* He stressed the fact that violation of the sacred marriage contract is nothing less than infidelity and adultery.

It is clear that here, as previously, Jesus went back beyond rabbinical opinions to the original intention of the law (Genesis 2:24; 24:6–7; Exodus 20:14; Deuteronomy 5:18; Malachi 2:14–16). Compare Ephesians 5:31–32 and Hebrews 13:4.

When we study Matthew 5:32 in connection with 19:3–9, we notice the phrase "from the beginning" in verses 4 and 8. The law made it very clear that in marriage one man is joined to one woman, the implication being that death alone is able to part them (Romans 7; 21; 1 Corinthians 7:39). The exception to which Jesus referred ("except on the grounds of infidelity") permits divorce only when one of the contracting parties—here, the wife, by means of marital unfaithfulness (adultery or fornication)—rises in rebellion against the very essence of the marriage bond.

An objection might be raised, however. Didn't Moses leave room for the exercise of a greater measure of freedom? Doesn't the regulation found in Deuteronomy 24:1–4 amount to this: if you wish to divorce your wife, go right ahead, but be sure to give her a divorce certificate? Such seems to have been the opinion of the scribes and Pharisees, though not all of them in equal degree, as the explanation of Matthew 19:3–9 indicates.

Actually, Moses had not encouraged divorce at all. While not completely forbidding it, he had greatly discouraged it. Indeed, whatever the meaning of the much-debated Hebrew phrase *erwath dābhār* ("some uncleanness"), when we take Deuteronomy 24:1 and Matthew 19:3 together, they most definitely discourage divorce. The regulation of the first four verses of Deuteronomy 24 may be summed up as follows: Husbands, you'd better think twice before you reject your wife. Remember that once you have put her away and she has become the wife of another, you cannot afterward take her back—not even if that other husband has also rejected her or has died.

Moses did mention the giving of a "bill of divorce" (Deuteronomy 24:1) but only in passing—that is, by way of assumption included in the warning. Scribes and Pharisees, however, as Matthew 5:31 indicates, placed all the emphasis on that certificate. In verse 32, Jesus placed the emphasis where it properly belonged. The religious leaders had greatly exaggerated the importance of the exception that made divorce possible. About that, they were always debating (Matthew 19:3–9). Jesus, on the other hand, stressed the principle—namely, that husband and wife are one and must remain one.

With respect to the translation of Christ's answer, commentators differ rather widely, particularly with respect to the words generally translated "causes her to commit adultery" or "makes her an adulteress." The reader must often have wondered how the act whereby the husband divorces his innocent wife could make her an adulteress! As if the disgrace of being unjustly rejected by her husband and forced to face the struggles of life alone were not enough, she was additionally to be branded an *adulteress*?

In reply, it is generally pointed out that the statement, when thus read, is being misinterpreted. It must be read proleptically: "she is called an adulteress because she may easily become one." Will the average reader actually so interpret the words, "Every one that putteth away his wife, saving for the cause of fornication, maketh her an adulteress"? Is not the real solution a better rendering of the original?

The Greek, by using the passive voice of the verb, states not what the woman becomes or what she does but what she undergoes, suffers, and is exposed to. She *suffers* wrong. He *does* wrong. To be sure, she herself also may become guilty, but that is not the point that Jesus is emphasizing. Far better would seem to be the translation: "Whoever divorces his wife, except on the basis of infidelity, exposes her to adultery"—or something similar.

What Jesus is saying, then, is this: whoever divorces his wife, except on the grounds of infidelity, must bear the chief responsibility if, as a result, she should immediately yield, in her deserted state, to the temptation of becoming married to someone else. The erring husband should be given an opportunity to correct his error—that is, to go back to his wife. This also explains the closing clause, according to which anyone who rushes in to marry the deserted wife is involving himself and committing adultery. It was thus that Jesus counteracted the loose morals prevailing in this day.

The more we study Christ's teaching as presented to us in this passage, the more we begin to appreciate it. Here, by means of a few simple words, Jesus discouraged divorce, refuted the rabbinical misinterpretation of the law, reaffirmed the law's true meaning (Matthew 5:17–18), censured the guilty party, defended the innocent, and throughout it all, upheld the sacredness and inviolability of the marriage bond as ordained by God!

The Woman's Freedom to Remarry

If divorce was allowed, so, evidently, was remarriage. The text (Deuteronomy 24:1) presupposes that, once the woman had been divorced, she was free to remarry, even if she was the guilty party, having done something indecent. In fact, so far as is known, the cultures of the ancient world all understood that divorce carried with it the permission to remarry.

Dr. James B. Hurley summarizes the marriage and divorce laws of the code of Hammurabi—who was king of Babylon in the early eighteenth century BC when Abraham left Ur—as well as the harsher Assyrian laws at the time of Israel's exodus from Egypt.

Dr. Gordan Wenham has added information from the fifth century BC papyri at Elephantine, a small Jewish garrison town in southern Egypt, as well as from Phelo, Josephus, and the Greek and Roman world.

All these cultures supply evidence for divorce by the husband, and in some cases by the wife, along with the liberty to remarry. Usually the divorced wife had her dowry returned to her and received some divorce money as well. If divorce was comparatively infrequent in the ancient world, it was because the termination of one marriage and the arrangement of a second would have been financially crippling.[138]

John and Mary's Story: Cohabitation

John and Mary both grew up with religious backgrounds. John's family was of the Methodist denomination, and Mary's was Baptist. Both had strayed from their upbringing. They decided to live together instead of marrying legally. Within a seven-year period, they had four children.

Their relationship was tumultuous. Mary had checked herself in and out of psychiatric wards, and John was a chronic alcoholic and womanizer. Mary decided she would have other men because she wasn't legally married. One day John came home and found Mary with another man. They had an argument. Mary left the home and was not heard from for ten years. Meanwhile, the children were placed in foster care.

John and Mary's story is a tragic consequence of the belief that cohabitation is better than marriage.

Let's explore cohabitation.[139] People may decide to cohabit for what they regard as the best of reasons. For instance, they may not wish to replicate the mistakes of their married parents, succumb to the materialism of expensive weddings, or reduce their relationship to a marriage license. What constitutes marriage before God is neither a legal document nor a church service. It is not an elaborate reception or a shower of gifts. Rather, it is a reciprocal covenant that pledges lifelong fidelity and is consummated in sexual union.

In light of this, some cohabitation may almost be regarded as marriage by another name, since the essence of marriage—a covenant commitment—is there. Nevertheless, two essential elements are usually missing. The first is the promise of a lifetime commitment. Cohabitation is too often an open-ended arrangement, a kind of trial marriage in which permanent commitment has been replaced by a temporary experiment. This cannot be called marriage. Moreover, its provisional nature is bound to destabilize the relationship.

Cohabitation Is Unstable

First, the period of cohabitation tends to be short-lived. Unmarried cohabitations overall are less stable than marriages. The probability of a first marriage ending in separation or divorce within five years is 20 percent, but the probability of a premarital cohabitation breaking up within five years is 49 percent. After ten years, the probability of a first marriage ending is 33 percent, compared with 66 percent for cohabitations.

Second, among women the probability of a first premarital cohabitation leading to marriage is 58 percent after three years of cohabitation and 70 percent after five years of cohabitation.[140]

These figures, however, are different when work status, educational background, and ethnicity are included. In the United Kingdom, around three in five cohabitations lead to marriage.

Third, the claim that a trial period will make a later marriage more stable is not borne out by the facts. "Those couples marrying in the 1980s, having first cohabitated, were 50 percent more likely to have divorced within five years of marrying than those who did not previously cohabitate.

Fourth, there is a greater likelihood within cohabitation that a partner, particularly a man, will have more than one sexual relationship. No relationship can be comparable to marriage if it does not include the intention to be faithful to one partner for life. "What God has joined together," Jesus said, "let no one separate" (Matthew 19:6).

Fifth, cohabitation is related to a series of dysfunctional indicators when compared to marriage. A study carried out in the United States shows that the lifetime prevalence of alcoholism, depression, and general mental illness is much higher for those who cohabit than for those who have an intact marriage.

Cohabitation Is Informal

In society, family and friends have a right to know what kind of relationship exists so that they can adjust to it. They would naturally also desire an opportunity to say good-bye, to celebrate, and to promise support in the future. It is neither fair nor kind to leave families in the dark and in the cold.

A solemn pledge can hardly be regarded as "binding" without the sanctions of law. Moreover, couples who commit themselves to each other need the protection that the law gives them. The public context for marriage is important, as the community witnesses the promises that the man and the woman make.

When a man and a woman wish to live morally together, they owe each other exclusive, lifelong faithfulness. This is the only moral context for sexual relationships. God calls them to faithfulness, whether or not they recognize this. Public pledges admit and recognize the moral obligation that God has already laid on them by virtue of their existing relationship. A couple's commitment needs to be public as well as permanent, and the role of the family, the law, and the churches make the difference between marriage and cohabitation.

The Difference between Fornication and Adultery

The term *fornication*[141] is very broad in meaning. In its widest sense, it indicates immorality or sexual sin in general, illicit relationships of every description, and unlawful sexual intercourse in particular. This would include bestiality and homosexuality. *Fornication* in the Greek is *porneia*, indicating all kinds of impurity, perversion, and immorality. In 1 Corinthians 5:1, Paul says, "It is reported commonly that there is fornication among you, and such fornication as is not so much as named among the Gentiles, that one should have his father's wife.

In 1 Corinthians 6:18, it says: "Flee fornication. Every sin that a man doeth is without the body: but he that commiteth fornication sinneth against his own body." All sins destroy, but he who commits fornication sins against his entire constitution—even his body, soul, and spirit.

The term *adultery* means sexual intercourse between a married person and another who is not that person's spouse. A person can be a fornicator without being an adulterer, but a person cannot be an adulterer and not be a fornicator also.

Fornication Allows for Remarriage: Tony and Angela's Story

When Angela met Tony, she thought he was the answer to her prayers. She was thirty-nine and had a ten-year-old son whose father had died four years earlier. Tony had recently lost his wife through death. Angela thought Tony's widowed state made him saintly and that she was lucky to get such a catch. Angela threw counsel and wisdom aside, fully trusting Tony's decisions. They were married within six weeks after meeting each other.

Angela witnessed what was an obvious and inappropriate interaction between Tony and a relative and confronted him on it. Tony admitted that it looked suspicious but insisted that it wasn't as it seemed. A year and a half into the marriage, Angela was informed by family members that Tony had exhibited sexually inappropriate behaviors toward two preteen girls.

Angela again confronted Tony's behavior. Tony cried and said it wouldn't happen again. Angela felt that Tony should be forgiven and given another opportunity to be a faithful husband. Angela asked Tony to seek counsel and accountability. Tony made an attempt but wouldn't follow through.

Another year went by, with another report of Tony's sexual harassment. Angela and Tony both decided it was time for professional counseling. Tony did not believe his behaviors needed to change and refused to see the seriousness of his behavior—until his victim refused to keep his secret any longer and reported molestation. By that time, Angela felt she could no longer trust that he would repent and filed for divorce.

In its more restricted sense, *fornication* denotes voluntary sexual communion between an unmarried person and one of the opposite sex. In this sense, the fornicators (*pornoi*) are distinguished from the adulterers (*moichoi*) as in 1 Corinthians 6:9. In a wider sense, *porneia* signifies unlawful cohabitation of either sex with an unmarried person.

In its widest sense, *porneia* denotes immorality in general, or every kind of sexual transgression. In 1 Corinthians 5:1, *porneia* is rightly translated in the Revised Standard Version as "immorality." While other sins must be overcome by spiritual crucifixion of the flesh (Galatians 5:24), the sin of immorality (*porneia*) is one from which the Christian must flee in order to keep pure (1 Corinthians 6:18). Since God's close relation to his people is regarded as a marriage bond (Ephesians 5:23–27), all forms of apostasy are designated in Scripture as adultery.

Among Jews,[142] a woman had just as much right to put away a husband as the husband had to put away a wife. A woman could say to the elders that her parents or brethren had deceived her by betrothing her to the husband when she was young. She could then state, "I now reveal to you that I will not have him as my husband." Some parted by mutual consent, and this was considered legal, as was also their remarriage to others. All divorces were considered the complete dissolving of the marriage bond, and consequently, they were free to remarry. Any woman or man who got a divorce on grounds other than this was allowed to remain single or to remarry the former companion. Divorce on scriptural grounds meant that a person was free to remarry, providing it was to another Christian (1 Corinthians 7:15, 27–28; Matthew 5:32; 19:6). The innocent were not to be held responsible for the sins of the guilty (Ezekiel 13:17–32; 18:2–4).

The Death of a Spouse Allows for Remarriage: Nelson and Martha's Story

Nelson and Martha met at church. Nelson was attracted to Martha the minute he laid eyes on her. They soon began dating, and after a yearlong courtship, they decided to seek marriage counseling, which lasted approximately eight weeks. With the blessing of their pastor, they married in 1993.

Martha and Nelson had the typical first-year adjustment but soon became bonded to one another, inasmuch as you couldn't say one name without referring to the other. Nelson devotedly carried out his marriage commitment to love, honor, and cherish, while Martha fulfilled her role in submitting, respecting, and loving her husband.

On their eighth wedding anniversary, Nelson shared that he had health concerns. He went to the doctor and was diagnosed with liver cancer. Nelson prepared his finances so that Martha would be cared for. Within three short months, Nelson died. Martha grieved over his death for five years. She couldn't conceive of remarriage. But as God would have it, she met and remarried another husband. What does God's Word say to Christians whose spouses have died?

Romans 7:2–3[143] says, "For the woman which hath an husband is bound by the law to her husband so long as he liveth: but if the husband be dead, she is loosed from the law of her husband. So then if, while her husband liveth, she be married to another man, she shall be called an adulteress: but if her husband be dead, she is free from the law; so that she is no adulteress, though she be married to another man."

With the death of a spouse, all marriage bonds are broken. The living spouse is free to remarry, but *only in the Lord* (1 Corinthians 7:39). Paul gave the Christian law on this and laid down a restriction that she remarry only a Christian man, not a heathen. Paul then gave the advice that she would be happier if she remained single—in view of the current conditions in the world for Christians. Paul by no means contended for celibacy but gave sound advice for the present distress.

The command of marrying only a Christian believer is to fulfill God's original purpose of unity and oneness in marriage. The Scripture asks the question, "How can two walk together except they agree?" Being married to an unbelieving spouse can create tremendous struggle. However, if the unbeliever is content to live with the believer, the believer should not seek to divorce the unbelieving spouse.

Desertion Allows for Remarriage

In 1 Corinthians 7:15,[144] it says, "But if the unbelieving depart, let him depart. A brother or sister is not under bondage in such cases: but God hath called us to peace."

Here we have another legal and scriptural reason for divorce and remarriage. If the unbeliever refuses to live with a wife or husband because of Christianity, and if he or she is determined to leave on this account, the Christian is not under further marriage bonds and is not held responsible or punished by requirement to remain single the rest of his or her life because of the rebellion of another. The Christian is to submit to the breaking of the marriage covenant under such circumstances.

Julie's Story

Julie and Bill had a long-distance relationship. Julie had no idea when she married Bill that he struggled with substance abuse. Bill was addicted to alcohol and pills. Bill often stayed away from home. He would go to work and not return until the next day. He would take jobs out-of-state and send money inconsistently to pay the rent. One day Bill announced he was leaving for good. Julie asked him to stay, but he chose to leave, and no amount of pleading on Julie's part would convince him to stay. Therefore, because of Bill's desertion, Julie was under no obligation to stay married to him.

Bonding and Premarital Sex

Many people engage in premarital sex in the hope that it will bring them intimacy, only to discover that they feel empty and unfulfilled. Often dubbed the "morning-after syndrome," this is when a person wakes up after engaging in sexual relations with another person, only to discover that the intimacy they thought had developed was not really there at all. Instead there are two people in a bed who shared pleasure with one another and were intimate sexually—but in no other way.

Bonding and intimacy are about far more than just sexual relations. True intimacy involves the emotional need and desire to share with a life partner and to be a part of the total experience of sharing each other's lives. While there is sexual intimacy involved, true intimacy involves every aspect of an individual's being.

Many people consider it old-fashioned to wait to have sex, and studies show that in today's society, sex becomes an issue in a relationship much sooner than it did twenty or thirty years ago. This does not necessarily signal progress, however. The intimacy needed to fuel a serious, committed, and loving marriage between a man and a woman who wish to spend a lifetime together takes time, effort, and patience to cultivate. Mutual respect and trust must develop between two people in order for bonding to take place.

It is important not to use sex as the determining factor for whether or not the relationship will survive. Bonding is intimacy, and that involves letting another person into our lives completely and allowing love, tenderness, warmth, compassion, acceptance, and a feeling of closeness to enter into our hearts and lives.[145]

Premarital sex is sinful; it separates one from God, as well as causes an artificial bond. This artificial bond can become dangerously controlling and harmful. We will now look at the subject of *domestic violence*—what it is and how to stop it.

Domestic Violence:
What It Is, How to Stop It,
and How to Recognize
It before Marriage

Here are some definitions of *domestic violence*:

- Domestic violence (also known as domestic abuse, spousal abuse, or intimate partner violence) occurs when a family member, partner, or ex-partner attempts to physically or psychologically dominate another (www.en.wikipedia,org/wiki/domesticviolence).
- Violence committed by one member of a family or household against another (www.en.wikipedia,org/wiki/domesticviolence).
- A pattern of physically, sexually, and/or emotionally abusive behaviors used by one individual to assert power or maintain control over another, in the context of an intimate or family relationship (www.halifaxprosecutor.com/definitions.htm).
- This isn't just hitting or fighting or an occasional mean argument. It is a chronic abuse of power. The abuser tortures and controls the victim by calculated threats, intimidation, and physical violence. Actual physical violence is often the end result of months or years of intimidation and control (www.co.mclean.il.us/dv/definitions.htm).

There are warning signs before marriage and within marriage that need to be recognized. Here are fifteen warning signs. If you are concerned about your relationship, talk to a trusted professional for advice and help.

Fifteen Warning Signs of an Abusive Relationship

1. *Pushing for quick involvement*: Your partner comes on strong, claiming, "I've never felt loved like this by anyone." An abuser pressures the new partner for an exclusive commitment almost immediately.

2. *Jealousy*: Your partner is excessively possessive, calls constantly, or visits unexpectedly. He or she prevents you from going to work because "you might meet someone" and checks the mileage on your car.

3. *Controlling*: Your partner interrogates you intensely (especially if you're late) about whom you talked to and where you were, keeps all the money, and insists you ask permission to go anywhere or do anything.

4. *Unrealistic expectations*: Your partner expects you to be the perfect mate and to meet his or her every need.

5. *Isolation*: Your partner tries to cut you off from family and friends, and accuses people who are your supporters of "causing trouble." The abuser may deprive you of a phone or car or try to prevent you from holding a job.

6. *Blames others for problems and mistakes*: Your partner thinks it's always someone else's fault if something goes wrong.

7. *Makes others responsible for his or her feelings*: Your partner says, "You make me angry," instead of "I am angry," or says, "You're hurting me by not doing what I tell you."

8. *Hypersensitivity*: Your partner is easily insulted, claiming hurt feelings when he or she is really mad. He or she rants about the injustice of things that are just a part of life.

9. *Cruelty to animals or children*: Your partner kills or brutally punishes animals. He or she also may expect children to do things that are far beyond their ability (e.g., whipping a three-year-old for wetting a diaper), or he or she may tease them until they cry. Sixty-five percent of abusers who beat their partner will also abuse children.

10. *"Playful" use of force during sex*: Your partner enjoys throwing you down or holding you down against your will during sex and finds the idea of rape exciting.

11. *Verbal abuse*: Your partner constantly criticizes or says blatantly cruel things and degrades, curses, or calls you ugly names. This may also involve sleep deprivation, waking you up with relentless verbal abuse.

12. *Rigid gender roles*: Your partner expects you to serve, obey, and remain at home.

13. *Sudden mood swings*: Your partner switches from sweet to violent in a matter of minutes.

14. *Past battering*: Your partner admits to hitting a mate in the past but says that the person made him or her do it.

15. *Threats of violence*: Your partner says things like, "I'll break your neck" or "I'll kill you" and then dismisses them by saying, "Everybody talks that way" or "I didn't really mean it."[146]

The Red Flags of a Potentially Abusive or Toxic Relationship

How a person handles anger when their partner disagrees with them tells a lot about the person. Do they make rude comments about the opposite sex? How do they describe the person in their previous relationships? Do they isolate the partner from his/her friends and family or accuse them of cheating when they're not?

Red Flags

- Abuses alcohol or other drugs.
- Has a history of trouble with the law, gets into fights, or breaks and destroys property.
- Doesn't work or go to school.
- Blames the partner for how others treat them or for anything bad that happens.
- Abuses siblings, other family members, children, or pets.
- Puts down people, including their partner's family and friends, or calls them names.
- Is always angry at someone or something.
- Tries to isolate their partner and control whom they see or where they go.
- Nags their partner or forces them to be sexual when they don't want to be.
- Cheats on their partner or have lots of partners.
- Is physically rough with their partner (pushes, shoves, pulls, yanks, squeezes, restrains).
- Takes their partner's money or takes advantage of them in other ways. Accuses them of flirting or "coming on" to others, or accuses them of cheating.

- Doesn't listen to their partner or show interest in their opinions or feelings. Things always have to be done their way.
- Ignores their partner, gives them the silent treatment, or hangs up on them.
- Lies to their partner, doesn't show up for dates, and may even disappear for days.
- Makes vulgar comments about others in partner's presence.
- Blames all arguments and problems on their partner.
- Tells the partner how to dress or act.
- Threatens to kill themselves, if the partner breaks up with them, or tells them that they cannot live without the partner.
- Experiences extreme mood swings: tells their partner they're the greatest one minute, and then rips them apart the next.
- Tells their partner to shut up, tells them they're dumb, stupid, or fat, or calls them other names—directly or indirectly.
- Compares their partner to former partners.

Other Cues That Might Indicate an Abusive Relationship

- The abused partner feels afraid to break up with the abuser.
- The abused partner feels tied-down, feeling they have to check in.
- The abused partner is afraid to make decisions or bring up certain subjects, fearing that their partner will be angry.
- The abused partner feels that if they just try harder and love the partner enough, everything will be just fine.
- The abused partner finds themselves crying a lot and feeling depressed or unhappy.

- The abused partner worries and obsesses about how to please their partner and keep them happy.
- The abused partner finds the physical or emotional abuse getting worse over time.

If you are an abused partner, you must open up and talk to someone. God wants his children in healthy relationships. An abusive relationship is not the heart of God. Jesus said in John 10:11, "I am the good shepherd that gives his life for the sheep." Jesus was always kind and respectful toward women.

A woman caught in abuse seems to feel that she has no other alternative—that she is not able to leave or get help. She/he may feel financially ill-equipped to support themselves and their children, and may also feel responsible for the abusive mate's behavior. They may also misunderstand the concept of the Christian family and the theology of covenant.

The God who created the heavens and the earth is a loving God. His name is Jehovah Elohim, the Creator God. God's creation is in loving harmony, and he provides for every living creature. He has created in mankind a will to choose, and he never forces his will upon us. He gives us instructions on how to treat one another in the Ten Commandments in both the Old Testament (Exodus 20) and the New Testament (Luke 10:27). *Sin* has marred the relationship that God intended for man at the beginning of creation.

When is separation necessary? Is a dysfunctional relationship acceptable?

The Massachusetts Department of Youth Services conducted a study on children who witness domestic violence (Sheila Y. Moore, "Adolescent Boys Are the Underserved Victims of Domestic Violence," *Boston Globe* (December 26, 1999): E7). These children are:

- Six times more likely to commit suicide.
- Twenty-four times more likely to commit sexual assault.
- Fifty percent more likely to abuse drugs.
- Seventy percent more likely to commit crimes against others.[147]

Canadian women with a violent father-in-law are at three times the risk for spousal abuse as women with a non-violent father-in-law (1993 Violence Against Women Survey).

Children affected by domestic violence may experience problems such as excessive fear, sleep problems, explosive outbursts, poor social interaction, poor conflict resolution skills, and other problems.

Research has shown that witnessing adult physical aggression is more disturbing to children than observing other types of adult conflict.

Children as young as one year old began to regress into states later diagnosed as "mental retardation" when they were exposed to parental hostilities that never went beyond the verbal abuse level. It is also important to note, concerning the question of contact with the abuser, that the symptoms of retardation quickly disappeared after the parents separated.[148] (Jack C. Straton, "What Is Fair for Children of Abusive Men?," *Journal of the Task Group on Child Custody Issues*, 4th ed. (Spring 2001).)

God's Response to a Dysfunctional Relationship with His People

1. God has a covenant with his people (Deuteronomy 7:7–11).
   - God is faithful in that covenant. Know, therefore, that Yahweh, your God, is God. *He is a faithful God*, keeping

his covenant of love to a thousand generations of those who love him and keep his covenant.

- God expects his people to be faithful to him. Yahweh said to Joshua, "Stand Up! What are you doing down on your face? Israel has sinned; they have violated my covenant, which I commanded them to keep. They have taken some of the devoted things; they have stolen, they have lied, they have put them with their own possessions. That is why the Israelites cannot stand against their enemies; they turn their backs and run because they have been made liable to destruction. I will not be with you anymore unless you destroy whatever among you is devoted to destruction" (Joshua 7:10–12).

2. God will divorce his people for abusing that covenant. "I gave faithless Israel her certificate of divorce and sent her away because of all her adulteries" (Jeremiah 3:8). "This is what Yahweh says: 'Where is your mother's certificate of divorce with which I sent her away? Or to which of my creditors did I sell you? Because of your sins you were sold; because of your transgressions your mother was sent away'" (Isaiah 50:1). "'Yahweh will call you back as if you were a wife deserted and distressed in spirit, a wife who married young, only to be rejected,' says your God. 'For a brief moment I abandoned you, but with deep compassion I will bring you back'" (Isaiah 54:6–7).

3. God confronts his people to call them to a healthy covenant with himself. Jeremiah 26:2–3 says, "Stand in the courtyard of Yahweh's house and speak to all the people of the towns of Judah who come to worship in the house of Yahweh. Tell them everything I command you: do not omit a word. Perhaps they will listen and each will turn from his evil way. Then I will

have mercy and not bring on them the disaster I was planning because of the evil they have done."

4. God reconciles only in repentance, e.g., Hosea and Jonah. To *repent* means to turn in one's thinking and to change one's behavior and attitude.
5. In the family, spouses are to be:
    *   Faithful to each other (Ephesians 5).
    *   Compassionate to each other (1 Peter 3:7). The husband's prayers are hindered if he does not live considerately/honorably with his wife.

God has called them to peace, and a spouse can confront dysfunction. If the unbeliever leaves, let him go. A believing man or woman is not bound in such circumstances. God has called us to live in peace. How do you know, wife, whether you will save your husband? How do you know, husband, whether you will save your wife? (1 Corinthians 7:15–16). Confronting abuse and allowing someone to leave may be what it takes to bring about repentance, but if not, you are responsible to care for your well-being and that of your children.

The Community Response to Domestic Violence

Rescuing the Victims

"Many voices declare that the church has either caused men to be violent toward their wives or at least provided fertile soil for men's mistreatment of power within their families. They argue that since the church is part of the problem, it cannot be part of the solution. Thus when violence against women is being discussed, God's people are seldom consulted. Since we speak out so infrequently about violence, our collective voice is never heard on this issue. Generally speaking, leaders in religious organizations and those involved in community pastoral care are never even invited to participate at the secular consultation table. The silence of our churches and our leaders is often interpreted in the public square is complicity with violent acts" (Kroeger, Nason-Clark, 16).

"As long as Christian theology and pastoral practice do not publicly repent their collusion in sexual, domestic, and political violence against women and children, the victims of such violence are forced to choose between remaining a victim or remaining a Christian" (Elizabeth Shussler Fiorenza, *Violence Against Women*, xviii).

Protecting the Victims

There are three times as many animal shelters in the United States as there are domestic violence shelters for women and their children.

Confronting Abusers or Holding Them Accountable

It is men's work to unlearn violence as a response to need, and to learn to acknowledge and express needs in healthy nonviolent ways, and to form relationships of intimacy and interdependence rather than dominance and control" (Pamela Cooper-White, *The Cry of Tamar*, 218).

Helping Abusers Repent and Change

The church must no longer be a part of the "good old boys club." She must stand for truth and confront abusers, demanding that they seek help.

Sources of Help for Victims of Domestic Violence

Most Helpful Resources

Another Christian woman in the church	69.8%
Christian woman	66.5%
Pastor/preacher	58.7%
Physician	35.5%
Christian counselor	24%
Police	8%

Preferred Methods of Support

Listening ear	91.9%
Friendship/kindness	27.2%
Lodging	22.8%
Prayer	12.5%
Childcare	12.5%

As we see from these statistics,[149] another Christian woman and ministers are among the most helpful to domestic violence victims. The preferred method of support is a listening ear. By knowing this, our hearts should be moved with compassion toward those caught in this dysfunctional, life-threatening situation. As the church, we need to take courage and support these victims with prayer, biblical counseling, and community resources.

When it becomes necessary to leave an abusive spouse or relationship, there needs to be a safety plan in place. The following section offers a helpful guide.

Safety Planning

Safety During an Explosive Incident

- If an argument seems unavoidable, try to have it in a room or area where you have access to an exit. Try to stay away from the bathroom, kitchen, bedroom, or anywhere else where weapons might be available.
- Practice how to get out of your home safely. Identify which doors, windows, elevator, or stairwell would be best.
- Have a packed bag ready, and keep it at a relative's or a friend's home in order to leave quickly.
- Identify one or more neighbors you can tell about the violence, and ask that they call police if they hear a disturbance coming from your home.
- Devise a code word to use with your children, family, friends, and neighbors when you need the police.
- Decide and plan for where you will go if you have to leave home—even if you don't think you will need to.
- Use your own instincts and judgment. If the situation is very dangerous, consider giving the abuser what he wants to calm him down. You have the right to protect yourself until you are out of danger.
- Always remember that you *don't* deserve to be hit or threatened.

Safety When Preparing to Leave

- Open a savings account and/or credit card in your own name to start to establish or increase your independence.

Think of other ways in which you can increase your independence.

- Get your own post office box. You can privately receive checks and letters to begin your independence.
- Leave money, an extra copy of keys, copies of important documents, extra medicines, and clothes with someone you trust, so you can leave quickly.
- Determine who will let you stay with them or lend you some money.
- Keep the shelter or hotline phone number close at hand, and keep some change or a calling card on you at all times for emergency phone calls.
- Remember, leaving your batterer is the most dangerous time. Review your safety plan as often as possible in order to plan the safest way to leave your batterer.
- When returning home, inspect the exterior of your house or apartment. Check your windows and doors. Check for any signs of forced entry. If you think someone has broken into your home, drive or walk to a neighbor's house and call the police.

Other Important Tips

- Consider buying pepper gas. The kind that you need to purchase is a 10 percent pepper gas laced with mace. While the pepper gas will disable someone, the mace will give you added time to run away or call police. A medium-size can is best. Also, try to stay away from ones that come inside a leather case; that way you won't have to worry about getting the snap undone. Last, but not least, buy one that has a stream, not a mist. With a mist, you run the chance of it coming back into your own face. Check your spray periodically.

- Also consider purchasing a cellular phone. Keep the battery charged and carry it with you at all times. If you feel uneasy, you may punch in the numbers 9-1-1. Most cell phones will keep that information stored. All you have to do next is hit the send button.

Safety and Emotional Health

- If you are thinking of returning to a potentially abusive situation, discuss an alternative plan with someone you trust.
- If you have to communicate with your partner, determine the safest way to do so.
- Have positive thoughts about yourself, and be assertive with others about your needs.
- Decide whom you can talk to freely and openly to give you the support you need.
- Plan to attend a women's or victim's support group for at least two weeks to gain support from others and to learn more about yourself and your relationship.

What You Need to Take with You When You Leave: A Checklist

1. **Identification**
   - Driver's license
   - Child(ren)'s birth certificate(s)
   - Social security card(s)
   - Welfare identification

2. **Financial**
   - Money and/or credit cards
   - Bank books
   - Checkbooks

3. **Legal**
   - Your order of protection/restraining order
   - Lease rental agreement/house deed
   - Car registration and insurance papers
   - Health and life insurance papers
   - Medical records for you and your children
   - School records
   - Work permit visa/passport
   - Divorce papers
   - Custody visitation papers[150]

Other
   - House/car keys
   - Medication/toiletries/diapers
   - Jewelry
   - Address book
   - Phone card
   - Picture of children, you, and the abuser

- Children's small toys
- Change of clothes for you and the children

Source: McLean County Domestic Violence Safety Planning, http://www.co.mclean.il.us/DV/Safety_Planning.htm

Restraining Order Laws in Washington and Oregon

It is important for pastors and those in the helping professions to know how to guide in legal protection, and the following are restraining order laws in Washington and Oregon.

Restraining Orders: Oregon

The Family Abuse Protection Act is the legal basis for a domestic violence restraining order in Oregon. The person seeking the restraining order must go to the court and complete a petition for the restraining order, describing the acts of violence that have occurred *within 180 days preceding the filing of the petition.* The victim must be in imminent danger of further abuse by the alleged abuser. If a temporary restraining order ("FAPA Order") is granted in favor of the moving party, it must be personally served on the alleged abuser before it is effective. Typically, the county sheriff will serve the temporary restraining order on the alleged abuser.

Once the alleged abuser is served with the FAPA order, he or she will have thirty days to request a hearing. If no hearing is requested, the order will remain in effect for one year. If children are involved and custody and parent time is an issue, the court will attempt to schedule a hearing within fourteen days of the request. The alleged abuser may request that the hearing be scheduled within five days from the date the temporary restraining order is issued.

At the hearing, the court will hear testimony and evidence from both parties regarding the allegations of abuse. If the court finds by a preponderance of evidence that the abuse has occurred, the FAPA order will remain in effect for one year. Otherwise, the FAPA order will be dismissed.

Restraining Orders: Washington

In Washington, the victim must petition the court for a Domestic Violence Order of Protection. If the court is satisfied that the allegations are severe enough that the victim's safety is in jeopardy, or that irreparable injury could occur from domestic violence if the order is not granted, the court will issue a temporary order for protection. The temporary order for protection is effective for fourteen days, during which time the alleged abuser must be served with the order. Service is typically completed by the county sheriff.

If the order is not served prior to the expiration of fourteen days, the temporary order for protection must be renewed by the court. If the temporary order for protection is served on the alleged abuser before the expiration of fourteen days, the parties are required to appear in court at the date and time indicated in the order.

At the hearing, the court will hear testimony and evidence presented by both parties. If the court finds that the abuse has occurred and that the victim is subject to irreparable injury from domestic violence, the order of protection will be continued for one year. The victim will be required to petition the court for an extension of the order beyond one year three months prior to the expiration of the order.[151]

The Effects of Divorce on Society: Government Neglect of Marriage

Married couples have been left out in the cold because of political correctness in the government's family policies, a new report suggests.

The amount of money invested specifically in support for married couples has fallen significantly in recent years, says a new report from the Christian Charity Care. In one year, the report found that more money was spent on support for same-sex couples than married ones. Meanwhile, specific references to marriage have been phased out in favor of general terms covering "relationships" with varying degrees of commitment.

Yet research shows that married couples are more likely to stay together and bring up happy, healthy children than are adults in any other kind of arrangement.

Cohabitation relationships are far more likely to break down than marriages, with disastrous consequences for any children involved. Yet worryingly, 44 percent of babies are born to unmarried parents.

The new report points out that while marriage—with its proven success rate—has been abandoned, the disintegration of stable family life is costing the government billions each year.

The Labor Party's 1997 election manifesto stated: "We will uphold family life as the most secure means of bringing up our children." But according to think tank Civitas, deputy Labor leader Harriet Harman believes that "marriage has little relevance in public policy" and said that there is "no 'ideal' parenting scenario."

The report's author, Dr. Dan Boucher, urged the government to increase specific funding for marriage support. He said, "We are struggling with increasing anti-social behavior in the context of family breakdown. The cost associated with weak marriage via family breakdown—which is, of course, picked up by the taxpayer—is estimated to be well over twenty billion dollars per annum, a huge drain on our economy."[152]

Effect on Government & Taxpayers

Divorce has an effect on many areas, whether it is intended or not.

When marriages fail, government grows. From cities and counties to states, to the entire nation, taxpayers are forced to pick up the enormous cost when families break down and become less able to care for themselves or to watch over their children. Well-intentioned government programs often subsidize negative behavior and contribute to the decline of marriage.

- Cost of divorce: each divorce costs taxpayers approximately $25,000–$30,000.
- Cost of family breakdown: divorce and out-of-wedlock childbearing costs taxpayers at least 112 billion per year in federal and state expenditures.
- Cost of prevention vs. picking up the pieces: for every dollar in taxpayer funds spent by federal or state governments to build healthy marriages and relationships, another one thousand dollars is spent dealing with the consequences of broken families.[153]

Impact on Businesses

Businesses also benefit from strong marriages.

- **ROI**: Return-on-investment studies have tracked financial gains of up to $6.85 for every dollar invested in employee wellness programs.
- **Savings**: Stress-related issues cost corporate America $300 billion annually, and failing relationships are a major contributor to employee stress. Happily married employees are healthier, have stronger immune systems, and handle stress better.
- **Profits**: Employees with healthy marriages tend to boost not only productivity and profits, but also company morale. They are more loyal, stable, dependable, and motivated, with less job turnover and lower rates of absenteeism.
- **Community relations**: People have a very favorable opinion of local companies that champion marriage.[154]

Impact on Adults

Adults are losing the many unique benefits of marriage:

- *Married people live longer, healthier lives.* The mortality rate for unmarried adults is 50 percent higher for women and 250 percent higher for men.
- *Married people are happier.* About 40 percent of married people report being very happy with their lives, compared with 18 percent of divorced, 15 percent of separated, 22 percent of widowed, and 22 percent of cohabiting people.
- *Married people are wealthier.* Married men earn 10 percent to 40 percent more than single men with similar schooling and job histories. Median household net worth is $132,000 for married, $35,000 for singles, and $33,670 for divorced individuals. Couples who stay married for life end up four times richer than those who never marry.
- *Married people avoid poverty.* Only 8 percent of those who finish high school and wait until they are at least twenty and married before having children live in poverty, compared with 79 percent of those who fail to do all three.
- *Married people are safer.* Single men are nearly six times more likely to be incarcerated than married men. Married women are far less likely to be abused.[155]

State-by-State Divorce Rates: Massachusetts and Nevada

Massachusetts and Connecticut rank first and second, respectively, for having the lowest divorce rates in the nation, according to 1994 divorce data from the National Center for Health Statistics. Both states experienced a moderate drop in divorce rates between 1992 and 1994 to remain at the top of the list. Massachusetts fell from 2.8 in 1992 to 2.4 in 1994, while Connecticut fell from 3.1 to 2.8.

Nevada once again had the highest divorce rate in the country, even though it experienced the most marked drop in divorce rates during the two-year period. Nevada fell from 11.4 in 1992 to 9.0 in 1994.

The divorce rate per one thousand population for the entire United States was 4.6 in 1994, down from 4.8 in 1992. Generally, rates were lower in the Northeast and Midwest and higher in the West and Southeast.

Only four states (New York, South Dakota, Missouri, and Mississippi) experienced a rise in divorce rates between 1992 and 1994. Eight other states held the same rate during 1992 and 1994. Vermont, with a drop in the divorce rate from 5.2 to 4.0, rose in rank from 27th to a tie for 15th position.[156]

1994 Rank and Divorce Rates for Each State

Rank	State	Number	Rate
	United States: 1,191,000		4.6
1	Massachusetts	14, 530	2.4
2	Connecticut	9,095	2.8
3	New Jersey	23,899	3
4	Rhode Island	3,231	3.2
5	New York	59,195	3.3
	Pennsylvania	40,040	3.3
7	Wisconsin	17,478	3.4
	North Dakota	2,201	3.4
9	Maryland	17,439	3.5
10	Minnesota	16,217	3.6
	Louisiana	***	3.6
12	Illinois	43,398	3.7
13	District of Columbia	2,244	3.9
	Iowa	10,930	3.9
15	Nebraska	6,547	4
	Vermont	2,316	4.1
17	Michigan	38,727	4.1
18	South Dakota	3,022	4.2
	South Carolina	15,301	4.2
	Hawaii	4,979	4.2
21	California	***	4.3
22	Maine	5,433	4.4
	New Hampshire	5,041	4.4

24	Ohio	49,968	4.5
25	Virginia	30,016	4.6
26	Kansas	12,093	4.7
	Utah	8,999	4.7
28	Delaware	3,385	4.8
29	Montana	4,153	4.9
30	Missouri	26,324	5
	West Virginia	9,179	5
32	North Carolina	36,292	5.1
	Colorado	18,795	5.1
34	Georgia	37,001	5.2
35	Oregon	16,307	5.3
36	Texas	99,073	5.4
37	Alaska	3,354	5.5
38	Washington	29,976	5.6
39	Mississippi	15,212	5.7
40	Kentucky	22,211	5.8
	Arizona	23,725	5.8
42	Florida	82,963	5.9
43	New Mexico	9,882	6
44	Idaho	7,075	6.2
	Alabama	26,116	6.2
46	Indiana	***	6.4
47	Wyoming	3,071	6.5
48	Tennessee	34,167	6.6
49	Oklahoma	21,855	6.7
50	Arkansas	17,458	7.1
51	Nevada	13,061	9

Source: Monthly Vital Statistics Report, Vol. 43, No. 13, October 23, 1995, Centers for Disease Control and Prevention/National Center for Health Statistics. All statistics are for 1994 except: California (1987),

Indiana (1987), and Louisiana (1983). Rates are per 1,000 population in specified area. All data are by state of occurrence rather than by state of residence (www.divorcereform.org/94staterates.html).

***shows that there are no statistics for those states at the time of recording.

With divorce rates steadily on the rise and affecting our families, our economy, and our children's well-being, the question arises: How can we fight to save our troubled marriages?

The following pages will explore possible solutions.

What It Means to Fight for Your Marriage

With divorce being the option taken by many individuals struggling through emotional pain, the question is: how can we fight for marriage? This is a deeply emotional question.

When a spouse commits fornication or adultery, it does not mean that one should automatically file for divorce. But because trust has been broken, it *does* mean that there is a need for intervention and accountability on the part of the offender. The couple needs to seek professional advice from a pastor, professional counselor, wise confidante, or godly layperson.

In order for the marriage to continue, there needs to be true repentance. The Bible says in Proverbs 28:13[157] that he who confesses his sins and forsakes them shall find mercy. The key words here are *confession* and *forsake*. To *confess* means, in essence, to agree with God that the behavior displayed was sinful and broke the heart of God and the heart of the mate. To *forsake* means to leave the behavior and carry an attitude of abhorrence toward the sin. It is only when we come to hate our sin that we choose not to engage in or repeat our actions.

Galatians 6:1[158] says, "Brothers, if someone is caught in a sin, you who are spiritual should restore him gently. But watch yourself, or you may also be tempted. Carry each other's burdens, and in this way you will fulfill the law of Christ."

The "Christlike" attitude we must endeavor to show the offending party is actually the love of Christ. To love a person is not to say that what he or she did was right or acceptable. But loving the individual means that we choose not to stand in judgment, understanding that we too are subject to the same mistakes apart from the grace of God.

Therefore, one of the ways we fight for marriage is through holding the offender *accountable*. This is a critical point in a relationship. There are offenders who choose to do what it will take to restore the marriage through counseling and rebuilding accountability and trust. Other offenders don't want to discuss their moral failure with anyone other than the spouse, saying they feel too ashamed. Shame is another form of pride. But the spirit of humility says, *I am willing to do whatever it takes to regain my relationship with my spouse and right standing with God*. There is great hope for individuals with this attitude.

In Psalm 51,[159] David said, "Have mercy upon me O God, according to thy loving kindness; according to thy tender mercies blot out my transgressions. Wash me thoroughly from mine iniquity, and cleanse me from my sin. For I acknowledge my transgressions; and my sin is ever before me. Against thee and thee only have I sinned and done this evil in thy sight: create in me a clean heart O God and renew a right spirit within me. Then will I teach transgressors thy ways and sinners shall be converted unto thee."

The first step in fighting for a marriage is to *meet with a nonjudgmental, Christian, biblical counselor and confess the sin*. When we bring what is in the dark out to the light, we allow the light of Jesus Christ to shine his love, forgiveness, and restoration in our hearts.

The second step is *communication*. There are verbal and nonverbal ways to communicate. In the movie *Fireproof*, starring Kirk Cameron, the father character challenges his son to do a selfless act for his spouse, once a day for forty days, in an effort to communicate love. In the section that follows this one, I have recorded some of my own ideas, which are not a replica of what was in the movie.

In his book, *Strengthening Your Marriage*,[160] Wayne A. Mack asserts that deep oneness can be achieved only where good communication exists. No two people can effectively walk together, work together, or live together without a good communication system.

The Scripture asks, "Can two walk together except they be agreed?" (Amos 3:3). Whenever you find two people who are continuously and harmoniously walking together, striving toward the same goals, conducting their lives according to the same standards, giving mutual assistance, and enjoying sweet fellowship with one another, you can be sure that they are in agreement.

Apart from our relationship to God, he intends the marriage relationship to be the closest of all interpersonal relationships.

To a large extent, a married couple's experience of genuine oneness will be determined by the health of their communication system. Nothing is more important to the development of genuine oneness than their union, communion, and communication with God in and through Jesus Christ. Therefore Christian communication is the basic skill needed to establish and maintain sound relationships.

Having emphasized the importance of a good communication system between the husband and wife, let's now explore how to go about building this system.

Openness and honesty in communication are essential to good relationships. God sets the standard by teaching us how to communicate through his example. God illuminates our minds to understand the Scriptures (Matthew 11:25; 16:17; 1 Corinthians 2:6–15). If God does not communicate with us, how can we really know him or have a close relationship with him?

When marriage breaks down, we can use the tool of *communication* to express our feelings. It may sound something like this: "I really trusted you. I feel betrayed and deeply hurt to the point of nausea, but if you are willing to repent and seek help, I'll be here. God is greater than my feelings right now, and his love is greater than your sin."

I am not suggesting that a couple must "tell it all." Scripture warns us that there are some things of which it is a shame to think or speak (Ephesians 4:29;[161] 5:3–4;[162] Matthew 5:27–28;[163] Philippians 4:8[164]).

Vulgar, crude, rude, and profane words and attitudes should be avoided. The following questions can be helpful in all our communication efforts.

- Is it really true? Do I really have the facts? (Ephesians 4:29;[165] Proverbs 18:13[166]).
- Is what I would like to say profitable? Will it help or hurt? Will it be constructive or destructive? (Proverbs 20:15;[167] Ephesians 4:29;[168] Romans 15:1–3[169]).
- Is this the proper time for me to say it, or would it be better for me to wait? (Proverbs 15:23, 28;[170] 25:11–12[171]).
- Is my attitude right? (Ephesians 4:15, 32;[172] 1 Corinthians 16:14;[173] Titus 3:1–2[174]).
- Are my words the best possible way of saying it? (Proverbs 12:25[175]).
- Have I prayed about this matter, and do I trust God to help me? (Proverbs 3:5–6[176]).

Good communication does not mean that a spouse should compromise with sin or evil in order to keep harmony in a marriage, as in the case of Sapphira going along with Ananias' wicked scheme. She should have lovingly admonished him and refused to cooperate in sin (Acts 5:1–11[177]).

Forty Days of Showing Love to Your Spouse

Day 1: Pray that God will soften your heart and take bitterness and a judgmental attitude away.

> Action: I will clean the bathroom and place a note inside the mirror with a Scripture verse.

Day 2: Pray that God gives you a heart of flesh, a tender heart toward your spouse, that you will see them through God's eyes.

> Action: I will wash the dishes or fold the clothes.

Day 3: Pray that you see your spouse as a person—not as a possession or object.

> Action: I will call my spouse by his or her given name. I will make coffee, tea, or breakfast.

Day 4: Pray for your heart to change and for you to see hope for the relationship.

> Action: I will read 1 Corinthians 13, the "love chapter."

Day 5: Pray that you will open your eyes to a practical need your spouse has, e.g., socks, underwear, a new razor set, or a dental appointment.

> Action: I will obtain what he or she needs.

Day 6: Pray that your spouse will come into a greater knowledge of who Jesus Christ is and will desire to be a faithful, committed spouse.

> Action: I will choose a gentle tone of voice and kind words.

Day 7: Pray for perseverance, even though your spouse may not think your motives are genuine. Pray for hope, even though things look hopeless. Reach out and talk with a biblical counselor.

> Action: I will wash the sheets and make the bed, placing a piece of candy or note on the pillow.

Day 8: Pray for honest communication with love and truth.

> Action: I will write a note affirming my love for my spouse and place it on the windshield of his or her car.

Day 9: Pray that God's purposes will come to pass.

Action: I will continue to speak kindly and lovingly. I will bless my in-laws in a way that is meaningful to them.

Day 10: Pray that God will change your heart and that you will offer forgiveness for the offenses done toward you. Choose to let them go.

Action: I will make my spouse a sack lunch for work.

Day 11: Pray for change in your heart, that you will see your spouse as a child, visualizing him or her in a wounded state, as a victim with no one to help.

Action: I will buy something that is significant to my spouse, no matter how small. I will send fresh flowers that look beautiful.

Day 12: Call a trusted biblical counselor and ask for prayer.

Action: I will offer to read a Scripture passage from the Psalms after dinner.

Day 13: Pray for continuance, and pray 1 Corinthians 13 aloud, replacing the word *love* with your name.

Action: I will cook dinner and set the table as if we were expecting company.

Day 14: Speak in terms of *us* instead of *me*.

Action: I will pray for my spouse to want our family and marriage above anything except God. I will get a gift card for my spouse's favorite activity.

Day 15: Pray that God will enable you to keep your marriage vow until death, not seeking another partner to fulfill your need.

Action: I will list ten sincere qualities of my spouse and e-mail them to him or her.

Day 16: Pray for the confidence to ask your spouse if you can read the Bible together at a specific time each day.

Action: I will run the bath water for my spouse and light candles.

Day 17: Pray that your heart will view your spouse through God's eyes.

Action: I will put away the groceries.

Day 18: Find out your spouse's love language: acts of service, gifts, words of affirmation, time, or touch.

Action: I will implement my spouse's love language today.

Day 19: Pray that God will help you to loosen up and laugh, that you will look at your spouse with a smile on your face.

Action: I will write and share ten things I appreciate about my spouse.

Day 20: Choose to be thankful that God is still in control and that he loves you. Read Psalm 23 prayerfully, recognizing that the Lord is your Shepherd.

Action: I will find humor throughout this day.

Day 21: Pray for your spouse according to Ephesians 1:16–19.

Action: I will buy a single red rose and place it on my spouse's desk at work with a love note.

Day 22: Read 1 Corinthians 13 today.

Action: I will wash my spouse's feet after dinner and put lotion on them.

Day 23: Pray for your spouse and read Philippians 2.

Action: I will offer support for any activities my spouse is part of.

Day 24: Choose not to be angry. Rather, respond in a "Christ like" manner. Pray that your witness for Christ stands, no matter what.

Action: I will seek out a small Bible study group to fellowship with.

Day 25: Endeavor to speak in tender tones to your spouse.

Action: I will pay for a massage or give a back rub.

Day 26: Remember to put Christ first in your life by having prayer and Bible reading, first thing in the morning.

Action: I will pray for my spouse's family members.

Day 27: Pray for your spouse's spiritual well-being.

Action: I will make lunch or take my spouse out to lunch today.

Day 28: Reach out and pray for spiritual help. Call or go to visit another Christian couple.

Action: I will make dinner for my spouse today and say that I love him or her.

Day 29: Educate yourself on God's blueprint for marriage by reading a book or taking classes on the subject of marriage and family.

Action: I will make sure the home is neat and in order when my spouse arrives.

Day 30: Repent to your spouse for not considering their needs above your own.

Action: I will get rid of material things that hinder my relationship with Christ.

Day 31: Understand that the husband-wife relationship takes priority above other relationships.

Action: If the opportunity arises, I will tell my family that the wishes of my spouse come first.

Day 32: Tell your spouse that he or she is beautiful/handsome to you.

Action: I will place a candy on my spouse's pillow.

Day 33: Arrange a trip to the mountains, coast, or beach.

Action: I will not answer my cell phone (except for urgent calls), realizing that this time is for me and my spouse.

Day 34: Make breakfast in bed for your spouse.

Action: I will ask if we may pray together and read Song of Songs from the Bible together.

Day 35: Speaking in a gracious manner, ask your spouse what he or she thinks about a certain topic.

Action: I will not be critical of my spouse's view. I will look in his or her eyes and listen attentively to the expressed viewpoint.

Day 36: Speaking in a gentle tone, ask your spouse what he or she needs you to do today that would be a great blessing.

Action: When he or she gives the answer—be it shopping, cooking, watching the children, cleaning the garage, or paying a bill—I will do it.

Day 37: Provide a fun activity for the evening, such as a decent movie, board game, bowling, theater, swimming, or a romantic dinner.

Action: I will pay a babysitter to watch the children if necessary.

Day 38: Seek out a marriage counselor/coach.

Action: With the permission of my spouse, I will arrange for marriage counseling to further strengthen our attempt to save our marriage.

Day 39: Pray and commit your marriage into God's hands, realizing that you must not worship your marriage but honor its covenants.

Action: I will reaffirm my commitment to my spouse today.

Day 40: Allow the peace of God, which passes all understanding, to guard your heart and mind in Christ Jesus.

Action: I will thank God for changing my heart. I will entrust my marriage to God, fully doing my part and expecting God's best!

Benefits of Professional Premarital Counseling

Premarital counseling is a form of counseling that can benefit any couple that is planning to wed. Premarital counseling is also called premarital preparation.[178]

It is important to remember that the word *counseling* can sometimes be misleading. Premarital counseling is not a form of therapy. Premarital counseling is educational and will help couples learn the skills they will need to support them in having a happy, healthy, and lasting marriage.

Premarital counseling will help a couple to identify and communicate their fears, desires, beliefs, values, dreams, needs, and other issues and baggage that have previously been avoided, denied, or overlooked.

Half of all marriages fail. Research has shown that premarital counseling helps to decrease the incidence of divorce by as much as 30 percent.

The belief behind premarital counseling is that it is necessary to encourage the strength of a marriage before it takes place and to prepare and anticipate challenges and conflicts that could arise in the marriage in the future.

Research into the benefits of premarital counseling has found that there is a window of opportunity that exists, during which a couple can most benefit from premarital education: the year preceding the wedding and the first six months after the wedding. As time passes and more stress comes into the relationship, a couple may find that negative habits and unhealthy relationship patterns can develop and become well established, which are very hard to break.

Research has illuminated seven areas of knowledge and relationship skills that help contribute to the development, success, and lasting quality of a happy, loving marriage. Premarital counseling sessions should address all of these areas in order to be of the greatest help to couples:

- Compatibility
- Expectations
- Personalities
- Families of origin
- Communication
- Conflict resolution
- Intimacy and sexuality
- Long-term goals

Premarital Counseling

The following is excerpted from the *Christian Ministers Manual* by Rod I. Huron, published by Standard Publishing in Cincinnati, Ohio, in 1984, page 118:[179]

Some couples only want to plan a wedding, but others are willing to talk about their lives together. These suggestions may be useful during one or more such sessions. Treat them as suggestions only; once the ceremony is decided upon, lay this manual aside and trust to God's leading.

Help the couple feel comfortable. The atmosphere should be that of friends getting together informally, not that of an authority figure issuing lifetime rules or an inquisitor probing intimate secrets.

The question, "How did you meet each other?" is a good opener and gets them talking about themselves and their relationship. Keep the talk flowing with genuine interest and comments, such as, "What did you think of him at first?" and "When did you start to be serious?"

The session moves to a deeper level with your questions: "How well do you think you know each other?" Laughing, they may ask, "What do you mean?" Help them explore their knowledge of each other with questions such as, "What does he/she like to do more than anything else? Where would he/she like to go on a vacation? What is something you do that really makes him/her unhappy?"

They can talk over their answers—sometimes seriously and sometimes not—and in the process learn even more about each other.

Has either party been married before? If there was a divorce, what led to it? Will that create problems in this marriage?

What will be their relationship to the former wife or husband and to any children? If the children from the former marriage will be in this new home, what steps will be taken to make them feel accepted and wanted?

There cannot be lingering doubts in the mind of one party concerning the past marriage of the other. Help them discuss these and clear them away.

What about health habits? Does either smoke? Drink? Use narcotics? How does the other feel about this?

Emphasize that marriage is not a reform school, that the ceremony itself will do nothing to change such habits. If there is a problem now with drinking, for example, it will not improve automatically after marriage. Ask, "How will you feel if he keeps on drinking after you've married?" If need be, force them to face this matter squarely.

Help them see the necessity of dealing with such issues now, rather than postponing making changes until later. If changes are not made now, in all probability they will never be made at all.

Ask, "Who will be the brakes and who will be the accelerator?" This opens up many possibilities about money, sex, work habits, etc., but the question is general enough that it enables them to bring up whatever area they want to discuss. Attitudes toward money, sex, and work habits reflect their personalities and emotional makeup. Who will be the more active? The more aggressive? Who is more likely to be passive?

Will there be a conflict if both husband and wife try to run the home? Is one person more ambitious or better educated than the other? Will this create resentment and cause a growing breach in their marriage?

Does he or she have a job? Does she plan to work after marriage? Will they have a place of their own, even if it is a rented phone booth in a bus station? If they are to live with parents, what will be the relationship with their in-laws? If the husband was to be offered a better position in a distant city, what would they do?

Who will handle the checkbook? Do they plan to have a budget? Which one will be the enforcer? And how strictly will he or she enforce? Are there debts that will create financial pressure?

Where do their families fit into their relationship? How do the families feel about the coming marriage? Does the couple see possible problems in this area?

How do they handle conflict? Has either seen the other angry? At him/her? What caused the trouble, and how did they resolve it? Who is usually the first to say, "I'm sorry"? Will he/she continue having to give in, or will there be mutual awareness when hurt has occurred, and willingness to back up, apologize, and go on? If this has not been the case up until now, why do they think things will be different once they are married?

The way conflict is handled now is "practice" for the way they will settle differences later. A problem here does not mean that this couple should not be married, but it does indicate that they need to develop better means of resolving their difficulties.

The following question opens up an important area, no matter the level of their physical contact, whether holding hands or living together: "Do you feel good about what is happening between you physically?" If they don't know how to respond, you may say, "Well, no doubt you're expressing your affection. I hope you're hugging and kissing each other. The physical aspect of a relationship is certainly one of God's gifts to a man and woman."

These questions can then go further: "Is one the aggressor? Does the other feel like the victim?"

They need to explore this area seriously, for the physical expression of love can enrich and satisfy, but the lack of adequate expression can frustrate and lead to resentment, outbursts of rage, illness, and divorce.

Help them see that love does not mean taking but giving. Do they hope to have children? How many? Have they discussed birth control? Do they have any health problems they need to discuss or take to a physician?

Will she plan to work if they have a baby? If not, will she resent staying at home? Do they intend to bring up their children in a Christian home? What steps are they prepared to take toward this goal?

Which one has the higher standards? Which one has the deeper commitment to Christ? How often do they plan to attend church? Where? How much do they intend to give to the work of Christ? Are they making these decisions now? What steps do they need to take in order to begin their marriage on a Christian foundation?

Offer to help the couple in any way possible as they approach their wedding day. Be positive about the wedding and the marriage. However, if serious concerns come to light, encourage the couple to deal with the issues head-on to prevent a divorce later.

Tough Love: Substance Abuse in Marriage

The following information is taken from Dr. James C. Dobson's Tough-Love Counseling.[180]

Question: If you were a counselor who was helping someone manage a crisis situation, your recommendations to exercise tough love could potentially kill the marriage. Doesn't that make you nervous? Have you ever regretted taking a family in this direction?

Dr. Dobson answers: Before I answer those questions, you need to understand how I see my situation. My role is similar to that of a surgeon who tells a patient that he needs a coronary-artery-bypass operation. The man sits in his doctor's office, hearing the probabilities of success and failure. "If you undergo this operation," the doctor says, "research shows you'll have a three percent chance of not surviving the surgery." Wow! Three out of every hundred people who submit to the knife will die on the table! Why would anyone run that risk voluntarily? Because the chances of death are far greater without the surgery.

The "love must be tough" confrontations and ultimatums are like that. They may result in the sudden demise of a relationship. But without the crisis, there is a much higher probability of a lingering death. Instead of bringing the matter to a head while there is a chance for healing, the alternative is to stand by while the marriage dies with a whimper. I'd rather take my chances today, before further damage is done. A blowout is better than a slow leak."

Moral issues must be confronted and dealt with head-on. Many individuals and families are struggling with substance abuse issues, which cause the demise and ruin of many marriages. We will now discover how substance abuse has affected our nation and what we can do to confront this pervasive problem.

Substance Abuse

Addiction is now the number-one public health issue in the United States. According to the US Department of Health and Human Services, in 2006 more than twenty-two million people needed treatment for addiction.

Addictions are powerful enemies, beginning subtly with an experience or substance that brings pleasure and then turning into an ugly obsession that controls and dominates the user. Rarely can a person escape the grips of addiction without some form of intervention and spiritual healing.

Here are some sobering statistics:

- 16 million people need immediate treatment for substance abuse.*
- 125 million Americans, age 12 or older, are current drinkers of alcohol.*
- 15 million of them are dependent on alcohol.*
- 500,000 alcohol dependents are between the ages of 9 and 12.*
- 20.4 million, 12 and older, use illegal drugs.*
- 43% of Americans have been exposed to alcoholism in their families.*
- 17,000 motor vehicle deaths annually involve alcohol.***
- In 2003, there were 1.3 million pornography websites: 260 million pages.*
- 47% of Christians say that pornography is a major problem in the home.*
- 10% of adults admit to Internet sex addictions, and 28% of those are women.*

- 43% of adult women and 25% of adolescents report using laxatives for weight control.*
- 3% of the US population is diagnosed with bulimia (binging/purging).**

Addictions are responsible for destroying individuals, families, friendships, relationships, reputations, and careers.

* 2006 National Survey on Drug Use

** Remuda Ranch

*** National Traffic Safety Administration[181]

Basic Information about Alcoholics Anonymous (AA) and Narcotics Anonymous (NA)

The following information was compiled by Kay McCrary, Education Director of Patient and Family Education at G. Werber Bryan Psychiatric Hospital in Columbia, South Carolina.[182]

How do I find an AA or NA meeting to attend?

Use the telephone directory. Both Alcoholics Anonymous and Narcotics Anonymous list local numbers in the white pages of the local telephone directory. When you call AA or NA, you will either be answered by a "twelve-step" volunteer, who will talk with you and give you the information you need, *or* you will hear a recording that gives the days, times, and locations of area meetings—plus the first names and telephone numbers of members you may call for more information.

What can I expect when I attend? What is a meeting like?

You will experience *fellowship*. When a meeting is handled right, you will come to care about the members of your group—and they about you. Relationships are an important part of wellness and life satisfaction. Through this fellowship, you will experience acceptance. You will be valued, not blamed. When you begin to try rationalizing a way to use again, someone will recognize what you're doing and will care enough about you to warn you and try to stop you. You will learn a great deal about recovery from both the advice and the mistakes of the members of your home group.

You will experience *hope*. By hearing the stories at the meetings and looking at the lives of other members who are recovering, you will come to recognize and believe that recovery is genuinely possible. You will gain hope and energy that will assist your recovery.

You will attend a standard meeting format based on the *Twelve Steps* and the *Twelve Traditions*. The meeting lasts for about an hour and opens with the Serenity Prayer. Each member of the group introduces himself or herself (for example: "I'm John and I'm an alcoholic."). If it is a *speaker* meeting, a speaker shares his or her recovery story. If it is a *discussion* meeting, there will be a discussion.

The meeting closes with the Lord's Prayer. Afterward, there is a fellowship time with tea, coffee, and conversation, plus an opportunity to look at, and maybe purchase, available literature. There is no charge to attend AA or NA meeting; a basket will be passed, and most people will put in a dollar, but it's fine not to put in anything if you don't have it to spare.

What is a sponsor? When and how do I get one?

A sponsor is a member of the AA or NA group, someone who has had a good recovery and is a teacher, advisor, and guide for another member who is trying to recover.

As in most life situations, you get out of AA/NA what you put into it. Ideally, a member should be willing to do "whatever it takes" to gain recovery and should try to "work the program" instead of just being a detached observer at the meetings. Having a sponsor is an essential part of "working your program."

Your sponsor should be the same gender as you; men sponsor

men, and women sponsor women. Get yourself a sponsor soon. You find a sponsor by listening to the speakers and finding someone whose recovery you admire and want your recovery to be like. Ask that person to be your sponsor. Do not be discouraged if she or he cannot. If it's taking you a while to locate a sponsor, ask at the end of a meeting for someone to be your temporary sponsor.

The Twelve Steps

1. Admit that we are powerless over our substance of choice, that our lives have become unmanageable.
2. Come to believe that a Power greater than ourselves can restore us to sanity.
3. Make a decision to turn our will and our lives over to the care of God as we understand Him.
4. Make a searching and fearless moral inventory of ourselves.
5. Admit to God, to ourselves, and to another human being the exact nature of our wrongs.
6. Become entirely ready to have God remove all these defects of character.
7. Humbly ask Him to remove our shortcomings.
8. Make a list of all persons we have harmed, and become willing to make amends to them all.
9. Make direct amends to such people wherever possible, except when to do so would injure them or others.
10. Continue to take personal inventory, and when we are wrong, promptly admit it.
11. Seek, through prayer and meditation, to improve conscious contact with God as we understand Him, praying only for knowledge of His will for us and the power to carry that out.
12. Having had a spiritual awakening as a result of these steps, try

to carry this message to other addicts, and to practice these principles in all our affairs.[183]

Alcohol and drug use are detrimental to healthy relationships, especially marriage. Husband and wives must seek outside help. The abusing party needs to seek support in order to stay clean and sober. Drug and alcohol abuse have lasting effects—on children especially. The acts done toward spouses and children during addiction may cause the removal of the children from the home by authorities. Therefore, it is imperative that the non-abusing spouse protect the children by requesting the using party to leave the home or by leaving with the children.

In the next few pages, I will deal with the topic of guilt and shame, as divorce brings up these emotions. Let's look at it from a biblical perspective.

Dealing with Guilt and Shame

The most tortured conscience can find peace.

She had been a stripper, prostitute, drug addict, and demon-possessed witch. It was hard to imagine a perversion or Satanic form of depravity she hadn't wallowed in. Two thousand years ago, Christ agonized on a Roman cross, shedding his lifeblood for those very sins. She continued in her extreme degradation until, finally, she joined herself to Jesus by faith, trading her wickedness for Christ's holiness. One day Jesus appeared to her and said, "You are a chaste virgin in my sight."

None of us has an infallible conscience. In fact, most of our consciences are at times wildly inaccurate. If you want scriptural proof of this, you'll find plenty:

- "My conscience is clear, but that does not make me innocent. It is the Lord who judges me" (1 Corinthians 4:4).
- "The heart is deceitful above all things and beyond cure. Who can understand it?" (Jeremiah 17:9).
- "This then is how we ... set our hearts at rest in his presence whenever our hearts condemn us. For God is greater than our hearts, and he knows everything" (1 John 3:19–20).
- "All a man's ways seem innocent to him, but motives are weighed by the LORD" (Proverbs 16:2).
- "There is a way that seems right to a man, but in the end it leads to death" (Proverbs 16:25).
- "Who are pure in their own eyes and yet are not cleansed of their filth" (Proverbs 30:12).

When facing guilty feelings, the most important thing is to

establish whether your guilt is real or imaginary. Tragically, most people stand guilty before God and are hardly aware of it. They wrongly imagine that if there is a heaven, they have a good chance of going there. On the other hand, there are countless thousands whom God regards as spotlessly pure and innocent, and yet they are riddled with guilt feelings.

We must clearly differentiate between deceptive feelings and spiritual reality.[184]

Feeling Guilty and Fearful before God

You have every right to feel guilty and fearful before God if you have not asked God's forgiveness for your sin and have not trusted Jesus to have paid the full penalty for that sin by dying on the cross for you. Christ alone is capable of the divine miracle needed to wipe out all guilt.

You are right to feel guilty and fearful before God if do not *want* God to take your sins from you. To refuse to be delivered from your pet sin is like a drowning man stubbornly refusing to let his rescuer drag him from the water. If you have no intention of giving up a particular sin, you'll die in that sin. The sins you love are as deadly as the sins you despise.

Everyone who is not trusting Jesus for forgiveness, or who does not want a sin-free life, is guilty before the Judge of the universe, regardless of how he feels.

If, however, you have met these two conditions—*wanting* and *asking for* God's forgiveness—his smile is upon you. Any pangs of guilt or fear you suffer are simply an illusion, like fearing there's an intruder in the house when it is only the sound of the wind. The feelings might exist, and they might be most unpleasant, but they are groundless. They have no correspondence to reality.

Let's briefly expound the conditions for spiritual cleansing. Then we'll move on to some exciting facts.

You must *believe* the Scriptures that teach that Jesus—and only Jesus—can remove your sin. He alone can pay sin's penalty, because he alone has no sins of his own for which he must suffer.

Once you put your faith in God, trusting that he is infinitely wise and good and always has your best interest at heart, the only logical thing is to resolve to *follow* his leading on every matter, regardless of how scary and costly it may sometimes seem. This is simply a decision, a state of mind. It means that, despite some sins still seeming attractive, you decide that God's way is best, and you sign over to him control of your life. It means refusing to enjoy the benefits of past sin: you will repay money you have stolen, not allow people to continue believing a lie you have told, and so on. And it means shunning the hypocrisy of wanting God's forgiveness while refusing to forgive someone else.

Sin's full penalty is death, and the sinless Son of God died for you. Why punish yourself? He's already taken your punishment! Are you morally bankrupt? No way! "Paid in full" is stamped over your every account. By joining yourself to Jesus, a divine exchange takes place in which Jesus takes your sins upon himself (that's why he died) and his perfection becomes yours. The holiness of Jesus floods your entire being, flushing out every trace of sin. That makes you spotlessly pure and perfect in God's eyes.

Almighty God can embrace you and delight in you as intimately as he does his own eternal, sinless Son. Every whiff of sin is obliterated, because Jesus died for your every sin. This central spiritual truth is expounded over and over in Bible. Scripture repeatedly promises this to you, but nowhere does it say that you will *feel* that it has happened. The whole of Christianity is about choosing to believe spiritual reality (faith) instead of your inner feelings.

It is worth prayerfully studying—and even memorizing—the

Scriptures, because this is a crucial area of spiritual attack. Just as Jesus was tempted in the wilderness and overcame that temptation by believing and quoting the Scriptures, so you will be tempted over this matter, and you can overcome by clinging to the dependable Word of God. Satan will disguise the true nature of the temptation, but it is actually a temptation to believe that God is a liar. The deceiver is trying to fool you into believing that God lied when he said that all your sins are forgiven, when Jesus said that all who come to him he will not cast out, and so forth. We must believe that God's Word is true, no matter how we feel.

The Guilt of Even the Nicest Person

No matter how horrendously evil you might have been, by God's standards you are no more guilty than anyone else. Scripture says that we were *all* dead in our sins. You can't get any deader than dead! Without exception, we were *all* a total write-off. "As for you, you were dead in your transgressions and sins" (Ephesians 2:1). "Made us alive with Christ even when we were dead in transgressions—it is by grace you have been saved" (Ephesians 2:5). "When you were dead in your sins and in the uncircumcision of your sinful nature, God made you alive with Christ. He forgave us all our sins" (Colossians 2:13).

Relative to each other, some of us seem fairly innocent and some seem very guilty. But this assessment is based on our own sinful standards. It's like someone who has murdered twenty people feeling superior to someone who has killed two hundred people. Perfection is God's only standard. We get just one shot at living a perfect life, and we have all blown it. We have all missed the mark. Whether we missed the mark by a millimeter or a kilometer means nothing. We all missed, and that's all that counts.

On the other hand, when you receive divine forgiveness through

Jesus, no one can be more forgiven than you. *Outside* of Christ, we all stand condemned, but *in* Christ we each stand spotlessly pure before the Holy One.

Simple logic suggests that our spiritual enemy, whom Scripture calls "the deceiver" and "the accuser," would muster all his evil cunning to distort this simple truth. If the Evil One wanted to keep people from the wonderful forgiveness that Jesus offers, he would try to convince them that they are not bad enough to need forgiveness. Or failing that, he would try to persuade them that they are so bad that they cannot be forgiven. Either way, the result is the same.

If he utterly loses that battle, and people become Christians, he then tries to get them to feel less sinful than others, producing bigots, arrogant fools, and hypocrites. For those resistant to this attack, he tries the opposite lie, hissing that they are too sinful to be fully blessed by God or to be mightily used of God. Either way, it renders a person powerless. It's obviously to the deceiver's advantage to make you feel that total cleansing is impossible for you. Don't let him get away with such lies.

If, after God has forgiven us, we won't forgive ourselves, we are implying that we have a higher sense of justice than the Holy One. Anyone having the impertinence to make such an accusation is on dangerous ground. We are also implying that Jesus is inadequate, that he didn't suffer enough for our sins, or that his holiness could not swallow up our sinfulness. There is no shame in a forgiven person *feeling* guilty. That is simply the deceiver at work. For a forgiven person to *believe* that he or she is guilty, however, is a concern.

The rest of this discussion assumes that you have made the decision to yield your present life and your eternal destiny to Christ.

Some dear people are so aware of the seriousness of sin that they don't feel it's right that God should let them off scot-free, and so they try to punish themselves. The most common self-imposed punishment is to deliberately feel miserable and to deny oneself certain legitimate pleasures for a period of time. This generally includes not allowing oneself the right to enjoy his relationship with God.

On the surface, it seems a noble thing to punish oneself for sin, and it indicates a strong desire to please God. However, it is important to realize that your life is not your own (1 Corinthians 6:19). You're God's child (John 1:12), and you belong to him. The way a parent disciplines his child is solely the parent's concern. Just as it would be wrong for you to interfere and punish someone else's child, so it's wrong for you to play God and try to punish yourself for your own failings.

Some people even punish themselves in the vain hope that it may help to secure their Lord's approval. But this only insults Jesus by implying that his death wasn't sufficient to gain your full forgiveness. Furthermore, believing you can help gain the Lord's approval by punishing yourself puts yourself in a spiritually dangerous situation. It is vital to your forgiveness that you place your complete faith in Jesus alone. Only Jesus is able to obtain God's approval of you, and so you must place no faith in your own futile attempts to please God.

Unforgiven sin separates us from our holy God (Isaiah 59:1-2). The sooner this rift is healed, the better. So, if you happen to sin, return to God straightaway, sincerely ask his forgiveness, and trust him for the strength to overcome that sin so that you will not commit it again. Once God has forgiven you, you are obligated to forgive yourself, because you should have God's attitude toward all things. To refuse to forgive ourselves is to imply that we have holier standards than God!

Exciting Facts

Let's explore some of the many wonderful word pictures the Bible uses to describe forgiveness. It could prove the most thrilling experience of your life.

Some of these word pictures were penned in the Old Testament, because in God's sight Christ was "slain before the foundation of the earth" (Revelation 13:8). They were written under the inspiration of almighty God, who knew how all sin, throughout all human history, would finally be dealt with by his eternal Son.

Your sins have been removed and taken away. "But you know that he appeared so that he might take away our sins. And in him is no sin" (1 John 3:5). "By this, then, will Jacob's guilt be atoned for, and this will be the full fruitage of the removal of his sin" (Isaiah 27:9). "The next day John saw Jesus coming towards him and said, 'Look, the Lamb of God, who takes away the sin of the world!'" (John 1:29). "And this is my covenant with them when I take away their sins" (Romans 11:27).

If you had a limb surgically removed, you might still suffer pain that seems to come from the missing limb. *Phantom limb pain* is the medical term. You would remember having that limb, but it is gone forever. It could still cause you pain, and yet it is no longer a part of you.

You may also remember your sins. Their presence can seem so real as to actually cause you pain. But despite what you feel, those sins are no longer part of you. They are gone forever. This is an important concept to grasp. Let it soak into the deepest part of you by taking time out to think about it.

In contrast to the removal of a limb, Jesus' removal of your sin does not leave you crippled. On the contrary, it heals you, like the removal of a tumor.

If you had a cancerous tumor, you would be alarmed; but if a surgeon said it had all been removed, you would have peace. You could not personally verify that every trace of cancer had been removed. You would have to take the surgeon's word. Your sins, more deadly than a tumor, have all been removed. The only way you can know this for sure is to take your Savior's word, and that makes it not only more certain that any surgeon's word but more certain than anything in the universe. Jesus' word has more authority than that of any other being in any world. His words spoke the galaxies into existence. He *is* truth. He, like no other, is utterly trustworthy. If he says your sins are removed, *they are removed!*

To the Hebrew mind, you could travel east forever and never touch west. "Your sins have been removed as far as the east is from the west" (Psalm 103:12). You were once in your sin. They were once part of you. But now God has placed an infinite distance between you and your sins. The memory might still be with you, but the sin itself is nowhere to be found.

"Search will be made for Israel's guilt, but there will be none, and for the sins of Judah, but none will be found, for I will forgive" (Jeremiah 50:20). "Your sins have been thrown into the depths of the sea" (Micah 7:18–19).

Almighty God trampled your sins under his feet, thus destroying them, and then banished them forever by hurling them into the ocean's depths. The Israelites' technology was such that anything below a few meters of water was utterly inaccessible. Anything dropped into the ocean depths was lost forever. No one would ever see it again. That's like what has happened to your sin. It's gone forever.

The holy Lord has given his word never to remember your sins. They have been erased, wiped out. "Hide your face from my sins and blot out all my iniquity" (Psalm 51:9). "I have swept away your offences like a cloud, your sins like the morning mist" (Isaiah 44:22). "Repent, then, and turn to God, so that your sins may be wiped out, that times of refreshing may come from the Lord" (Acts 3:19).

Your sins are not remembered. "I, even I, am he who blots out your transgressions, for my own sake, and remembers your sins no more" (Isaiah 43:25). "For I will forgive their wickedness and will remember their sins no more" (Hebrews 8:12). The latter verse is repeated in Jeremiah 31:34 and Hebrews 10:17.

You no longer need try to justify your past or apportion blame, because it is totally erased from heaven's data banks.

How to Survive Divorce
on Biblical Grounds

In his book, *Single, Married, Separated, and Life After Divorce*,[185] Myles Munroe talks about the traumas of divorce. His writing provides the basis for the discussion in this chapter.

"Two things are involved in divorce: the tearing apart of emotional bonding and separation distress.

Everyone has been involved in some kind of relationship that has failed—from kindergarten on up through adulthood. In the failing, some of those broken relationships left scars or even sores that have not healed.

A trauma is an injury, a wound, or a shock. It amounts to an earthquake to the systems of the body, soul, or spirit. Broken relationships always result in traumas, great or small.

Traumas cause distress, and distress manifests in anxiety. When you begin to be anxious, quite often you become at least somewhat irrational. Being irrational means that you begin to act without thinking properly.

The first thing that happens after a break in the emotional bond is distress. Separation brings distress of the soul. The first hurt is intense and sharp, caused by the tearing apart of bonds.

The distress includes all of the things you go through after the tearing apart: first, the wound, and then, the trauma.

Psalm 18:6 says, "In my distress, I called upon the Lord." Call first upon the Lord when you get caught in a traumatic situation.

Distress involves the same feeling of bereavement that follows the death of someone close to you. The same pattern that occurs after a loss in death also occurs after a loss of relationship."

Manifestations of Grief:

- Feeling physically drained
- Out of emotional control—feel good one minute; in the pits the next
- Can't eat—food makes you sick, people tend to lose up to forty pounds or they can overeat
- "Zombie effect" feeling shut down due to your body's natural coping mechanism
- Brain seems scrambled; can't think clearly or remember things, short term memory loss
- Can't cry—bottled up emotions —sometimes comes out years later
- Can't sleep at night
- Take naps frequently and are constantly tired
- Talk about it over and over and dwell on it every moment
- Lose interest in work, house, and physical appearance
- Think you will never recover from your loss
- Fantasize about the past
- Have lots of guilt about the things you did or didn't do
- Suffer from severe depression

There are five stages of grief:

- **Denial-Isolation**: can't believe the loss is real, feels like a horrible nightmare has occurred, want to withdraw and be alone
- **Anger**: blame God, self, and others
- **Bargaining**: God if you give me one more chance I'll change

- **Depression**: see's no future—can't ever imagine meeting someone to walk through life with again
- **Acceptance**: has come to terms with the truth of the loss, has accepted self and God's strength as enough to go forward

There is no set timetable for the grief process to end. The first four stages can intermingle. Most professionals agree it takes a minimum of at least two years to heal after a divorce or death have occurred. It is unwise to begin a new relationship under the said amount of time.

Even after the ending of relationships—whether it is through divorce or death—separation leaves wounds and a feeling of loss.

This author recounts "going to bed at night, mourning—or at any rate, feeling a loss. Overnight, somehow, my mind would forget for a period of time. When I awakened for a few seconds I felt ok, and then the thought of the event hit me in the pit of my stomach with deep and intense pain, allowing me to become freshly aware of my grief." Even those coming out of unhappy marriages go through the stages of grief to a certain degree.

After I counseled a woman who had divorced her husband on biblical grounds, (an "un-repented adulterer"), the woman said, "I know he didn't treat me well, even when he would come home late or sometimes not at all; but I still have feelings for him." The husband had had multiple affairs and treated her abusively until finally she had had enough.

Whether it is a positive or negative relationship—all broken emotional bonds result in pain.

Another stage of grief is depression, which is caused by the dramatic changes that you are experiencing; you thought things were going to be a certain way for the rest of your life, but are hurt because of the way they are actually panning out now.

Following a separation is the disappointment that hits one or both parties. They begin to reflect on all the plans and dreams they had together realizing the future they had once hoped for will not come to pass.

It is important for you to stay close to God through reading the Bible, praying, journaling and fellowshipping with other Christians, or you could wind up feeling debilitated. Depression stems from feeling rejected. Even the one who sought the divorce feels rejected. You may think, *I have been rejected, and the future I planned cannot come to pass.*

Ephesians 1:6 says something beautiful about rejection: "He hath made us accepted in the beloved." That knowledge is your comfort.

Many people, even Christians, walk around in depression for years after a broken relationship, grieving their hurt. Some women and men sometimes spend the rest of their lives confined to their homes.

You need to remember that separation is just an event, an incident. It is not the end of your life. Even the death of the other person does not mean your death. Losing someone forever through death or divorce does not mean that your life is over.

Heartbreak is a terrible experience. Sometimes your heart literally feels as if it is being crushed. Broken hearts are real.

Jesus said in Luke 4:18 that he had come to mend broken hearts, among other things. A broken heart also means a crushed spirit, and life seems to stop. You feel you are walking on top of your head, nothing is normal. You see the world through different eyes; your world is not the same. All of these things could result in death of some sort.

If you choose not to get out of bed and go to work, your mortgage/rent will not be paid. If you choose not to fellowship with others, you will become isolated and die socially. And of course, if you choose not to eat, you will physically die.

A crushed or broken spirit is dealt with in the book of Proverbs.

"A merry heart doeth good like a medicine; but a broken spirit drieth the bones" (Proverbs 17:22). "A merry heart maketh a cheerful countenance, but by sorrow of the heart the spirit is broken" (Proverbs 15:13). You may think it is cruel to ask someone to be merry or happy during such a horrible time in life. However, you have a choice to make whether to live or to die.

A broken spirit dries up your bones. Proverbs 18:4 says, "Who can bear a crushed spirit?"

There are many people who have committed emotional or mental suicide deciding never to emotionally bond again. They never make a try at another relationship again. It hurts too much. Others believe they can trust no one. The hurt has resulted in an expectation of being wounded again.

The antidote for the poison of divorce is found in Psalms 43:5: "Why art though cast down, O my soul? And why are thou disquieted within me? Hope in God: for I shall yet praise Him, who is the health of my countenance, and my God."

To regain hope again, place your expectation in God, not in man. Begin to praise the Lord for everything you can think of. Start with the gift of your life, even though you may not see hope in the future, God does have a plan for you. Isaiah 54:4 says "Fear not; for thou shalt not be ashamed" Make a conscience choice to praise God with your voice and your hands lifted up. If you have never done this, it may seem awkward at first, but what you are saying with your body is "by faith, I am praising you, God I am in pain, but I realize that you are the only one who can heal my pain and restore my soul." David said in (Psalm 23:3) "He restores my soul." The soul is comprised of the "Mind, Will, and Emotions." When you begin to worship, God's healing is taking place in all three areas. He is healing your "Mind," your thoughts will become clearer. He is healing your "Will," you will begin to choose life, and He is healing your "Emotions," your heart will begin to feel hopeful, and the event of divorce/death won't be preeminent. God's presence will be! Praising God does miracles toward restoring a merry, happy heart. Jesus is your life.

Psalm 34:17–19 says, "When the righteous cry, no matter how many afflictions, the Lord will deliver them out of their troubles."

The Reaction of the Church

Divorce hurts the members of the body Christ, and there are many mixed feelings. Some people try to analyze what the problems could have been. Some are genuinely concerned about the welfare of the family due to the implications of divorce on society.

There are those who believe that a divorce means you have failed, and have become a second-class citizen. There are churches where, if you get a divorce, the church rejects you, as well as your friends. If you are a minister, you can never get in the pulpit again. If you are an attractive divorced woman, the married women tend to become much more protective of their husbands in your presence, and your social calendar may not be filled as before.

Also, there are many churches that never teach on divorce, because they do not know what to say, fearing that if they do speak on the subject they may be actually advocating divorce. Because of the silence in the pulpit on this issue, individuals and marriages are suffering, leaving the parishioners to figure it out on their own. Today, three out of four marriages end in divorce in most Western societies, which means that most congregations have hurting people sitting there. It is very hurtful to go through a trauma-like divorce and to receive a cold shoulder from the people who claim to be warm with the love of God. That is not practicing the love of Jesus Christ.

There is only one unpardonable sin, and divorce is not it. Yes, divorce is wrong, but so are judging, slander, and choosing not to forgive the offenders. Divorce does not mean eternal damnation, and neither does remarriage.

Those who have never experienced the trauma that results from a broken relationship of the magnitude of divorce should be thankful and grateful to God Almighty. And they should not pass judgment and condemnation on those who have. Yes, God hates divorce, and divorce is defection or "backsliding" on a commitment. But God loves the divorcee and declares that he himself is married to the backslider.

Working through the trauma of divorce

Your marriage may have failed, but God does not call you a failure. Never confuse who you are with what you have done. Measure your personal worth by the fact that God gave you value before anyone ever met you. He loved you so much that He sent his son Jesus to redeem you, even if you had been the only person on earth! The following are some typical ways of reacting to the aftermath of divorce.

Isolation

One of the immediate signs of those hurt by the separation of divorce or death is to become isolated. However, by withdrawing into yourself, you are building walls so that no one can come in and you cannot get out. You become a prisoner of yourself.

In Genesis 2:18, God says to Adam, "It's not good for man to be alone."

Worshipping the Creature and not the Creator

When we are in pain we look for someone or something to provide comfort for ourselves. Many people medicate pain through other people.

This is a very dangerous thing to do. This is where remarriage or a "rebound" relationship occurs. This person usually has a point to prove, they are angry; it could be at the church, the former spouse or the way things have turned out. They throw caution to the wind and become reckless in their behaviors, bouncing from one relationship to another, going out with or perhaps sleeping with anyone just to prove a point to the former spouse which is: "I don't need you; I can always find somebody to love me."

Another way a person may try to handle the trauma of divorce is by trying to hang on to the previous relationship (not understanding that when it is over it needs to be definite). He or she may try to keep the one who left as a "friend" or to maintain contact on some other basis such as scheduling family vacations together. Former husbands may drop in to see if their ex- wives need something fixed. Former wives may need things fixed, or they may need to talk about the children, and so forth. When these lines are blurred there will be confusion and jealousy in the long, especially when one of the two decides to move forward and eventually remarries someone else. If there are children involved they will be impacted even more due to the dysfunction of this kind of relationship. Children naturally want to see their biological parents together.

Replacing the job for the Spouse

Some people throw themselves into a job or career and become workaholics. Work becomes their security blanket. It is a stabilizing factor. When employees are successfully pleasing their employers, or business owners are able to satisfy their clients, their jobs/career may become their source of identity. While work can be therapeutic to some degree, excessive work may mask the real pain of the divorce, causing emotional problems down the road.

What happens if the job fails or when retirement comes? The trauma from the failed relationship will be exposed.

Sooner or later, wounds have to be healed; they can only be healed by the appropriate attention. Covering a deep wound with a small bandage will not promote healing in the long run. However, investing in counseling or group therapy could help to bring about the recovery needed to move forward.

Divorce Recovery Self-Care tips:

To be healed from trauma, you must regain custody of yourself.

- **Make time each day to nurture yourself.** Help yourself heal by scheduling daily time for activities that you find calming and soothing. Go for a walk in nature, listen to music, light candles, and enjoy a hot bath, read the Bible. This requires finding a balance, setting priorities, and dealing with emotions—not repressing them but dealing with them.
- **Pay attention to what you need.** Firstly, as time goes on, the situation must be accepted, not denied, no matter how it hurts. Secondly, you need to get counsel before making any decisions—counsel from God's Word, from the Holy Spirit in prayer, and from people you can trust. During this time be focused on what you need. It is okay to say no without guilt.
- **Stick to a routine.** A divorce can disrupt almost every area of your life, amplifying feelings of stress, uncertainty and chaos. Getting into a regular routine of rising early in the morning to seek Gods' presence will provide a comforting sense of structure and normalcy.

- **Take a time out.** Try not to make any major decisions in the first few months after a separation or divorce, such as staring a new job or moving to a new city, or selling your home. If you can, wait until you are feeling less emotional so that you can make better decisions.
- **Avoid using alcohol, drugs, or food to cope.** When you are in the middle of trauma you may be tempted to do anything to relieve your feelings of pain and loneliness. But using alcohol and drugs or food as an escape is an unhealthy and destructive way of dealing with painful feelings.
- **Explore new interests.** A divorce is a beginning as well as an end. Take the opportunity to explore new interests and activities. Pursuing fun new activities give you a chance to enjoy life in the here and now, rather than to dwell on the past.

Recovery means the restoring of your soul. You must take responsibility for restoring your life according to God's original purpose and submit to His healing process. You can only find His purpose for your life by intentionally seeking Him; this will prove to be the most healing thing you can do to begin again.

Learning important lessons from a divorce

An emotional crisis provides an opportunity to learn and grow. You may be feeling emptiness in your life at this moment, but it does not mean that progress is not being made. Consider this as a period of reflection—a time out, a time for sowing the seeds for new growth. You may emerge from this experience knowing God better as well as yourself, resulting in a stronger you.

The apostle Paul understood this when he wrote: "But this one thing I do, forgetting those things which are behind, and reaching forth unto those things which are before" (Philippians 3:13).

In order to fully accept a divorce and move forward you need to understand what happened and acknowledge the part you may have played. It is important to understand how the choices you made affected the relationship. Truly learning from your mistakes is one of the major keys to not repeating them.

Some questions to ask yourself:

- Step back and look at the big picture. How did you contribute to the problems of the relationship?
- Do you tend to repeat the same mistakes or choose the wrong person in relationship after relationship?
- Think about how you react to stress and conflicts. Could you act in a more constructive way?
- Consider whether or not you accept other people the way they are, not the way they could or "should" be.
- Examine your negative feelings as a starting point for change. Are you in control of your feelings, or are they in control of you?

You will need to be honest with yourself during this part of the healing process. Try not to dwell on who is to blame or beat yourself up over your mistakes. As you look back on the relationship, you have an opportunity to learn more about yourself, how to relate to others and the problems you need to work on. If you are able to be honest with yourself by allowing the Holy Spirit to change your heart, you will have a better chance of having a healthy relationship in the future.

Why is forgiving important to Divorce Recovery?

The key to healing is *forgiveness*.

Choosing not to forgive is <u>not</u> an option. Oftentimes when people experience the deep trauma that comes with divorce they have one of two choices. To either become bitter or to become better people. Someone once said "choosing not to forgive is like drinking the poison, you intended for the other person."

- Choosing not to forgive makes a person bitter
- Choosing not to forgive can create unexplained anger
- Anger and bitterness negatively affect the relationships around us
- It takes away the mental energy needed to cultivate loving and healthy relationships
- Choosing not to forgive blocks our relationship with God

What does Jesus say?

("Matthew 6:14-15") For if ye forgive men their trespasses, your heavenly father will also forgive you. But if ye forgive not men their trespasses, neither will your heavenly father forgive your trespasses.

Some respond to that Scripture by saying "that's not fair; somebody has to pay for the pain inflicted on me." I have good news for you. Someone has paid the price for the pain and sorrows inflicted upon you. His name is Jesus. **Jesus has paid the debt in full.** We too owe a debt; you and I have been guilty of inflicting pain on others as well.

Forgiveness is simply letting go of the offense, and committing the offense to God. It is an act of the will, out of obedience you can choose to forgive the people who have wronged you. Forgiveness is not synonymous with trusting the offending party, trust must be regained. But forgiveness is what our Lord commands us to do toward our fellow human beings on this earth. I would suggest that you meet with a Bible believing pastor to discuss this issue of forgiving, if this is a struggle for you. In the meantime remember that the words of Jesus are always true and trustworthy.

Moving from Divorce to Remarriage

Remarriage is challenging in the best of situations. While most people are very excited about the idea of remarrying, very few adequately prepare themselves for the minefield of challenges that lie in wait for them. They should! Believe it or not, the remarriage divorce rate is at least 60 percent.

Today, let's take a look at seven of the most important questions to ask yourself and your partner before you start moving full steam ahead with the wedding plans.

1. How long have we dated?

Remarriage research shows us that, the longer the dating period, the more successful the marriage. Most remarriages happen quicker than first marriages. Typically, the rule of thumb for first marriages is to date at least a year. There's a lot more work that remarrying couples need to do, and there are a whole lot more players involved. Dating longer gives both of you the time to get to know one another, help any children adjust, and get you past that really early time in relationships when you're blindly in love and may overlook any faults that your partner may have.

2. How long have I been divorced?

Again, most remarriage research suggests that waiting a period of at least two years before remarrying allows for the greatest chance of success. I know you may be thinking, *Two years!* However, take a minute and think about it. There are a lot of tasks you need to complete before you're ready to make another commitment to marriage.

3. How well do my children know my new partner?

Your remarriage will be a *huge* change for your children. This means bringing a new person into their lives, whether they want this person or not. Their reaction to this person will have a major impact on your marriage. It's in your best interest for your children to meet this person only after at least three or four months of courtship. All of you should spend time together to get a feel for what that new life will be like.

4. How do I know if my kids are ready?

Divorce or death of a parent can be an extremely traumatic situation for your children. Think about how you, as an adult, experienced the situation. You have ways of coping that you have learned over the years. As children, they've not had the opportunity or ability to learn those yet. Most researchers agree that children are typically one step behind their parents in the grief process. What does this mean? It means that just about the time you let the kids know you are planning to remarry; they are finally becoming comfortable with single-parent life.

5. Am I emotionally ready to move on?

A remarriage, by definition, means that a loss has occurred, whether by divorce or death. Those losses need to be thoroughly reviewed and dealt with. If there are "ghosts" from the past, they will constantly haunt your new marriage and leave it vulnerable. Also, if you are still hurt from what happened in the past, you won't be able to make partner choices as effectively as you would if you were healed.

6. What do we need to know about being a part of a stepfamily?

This is critical. Stepfamilies are *not* nuclear families. They involve completely different dynamics. Without being armed with this knowledge before the wedding, you are setting yourselves up for failure. You don't get time to learn as you go, because those dynamics will be in full force after the *I-do's*. If you've not taken the time to educate yourself beforehand, you will be playing catch-up while you try to deal with the everyday stressors of being newlyweds.

7.   What do my partner and I expect from this marriage?
This is an important exercise in first marriages, but doubly so with a remarriage. One of the best ways to get at this information is to talk about how things were done—or not done—in your previous marriage and how you felt about it.

My hope is that, at the very least, these seven tips will get you thinking and talking seriously about the realities of remarriage. It's not all gloom and doom, but the honest truth is that it's tough. Without adequate preparation, the odds are against you, no matter how strong you think your relationship is right now.

Knowing the questions is the first step. Are you ready to really *understand* and, most importantly, *apply* the answers to your unique situation? Are you ready to achieve remarriage success?[186]

Making Better Choices

Whether or not a person has had a fantastic marriage and is grieving the loss of a spouse or is walking through a painful separation by divorce, we all have to be responsible for the choices we make. When looking for a new partner, how do we choose well? What are the characteristics of a healthy partner?

What to Look For in a Man

- Will he make a virtuous father?
- Will he be a steadfast and good leader, protector, and provider?
- Will he, be a good disciplinarian with the gentleness of a father who is strong and will teach his children by both word and example?
- Will he teach the children to respect their mother?
- Does he realize that marriage is a covenant relationship for life?

What to Look For in a Woman

- Will she make a virtuous mother?
- Will she be a good homemaker?
- Will she recognize the man as the head of the home and teach the children to respect his role by her words and example?
- Does she realize that marriage is covenant relationship for life?

Robinson and Blanton (1993) stated that the key elements for enduring marriages involve intimacy, commitment, communication, congruence, religious faith, adherence to traditional values, and religiosity. These are followed by educational attainment and professional status.

Traits of a Psychologically Healthy Person

Many people have asked what a psychologically and spiritually healthy person looks like. There probably are many opinions on this, but here are a few traits that I believe are helpful in identifying a healthy person. This is written from a Christian perspective, but I believe these traits will generally apply to all individuals, regardless of their religious preferences.

1. A healthy person has entered into a personal relationship with God through his Son, Jesus Christ. This relationship allows a person to be spiritually healthy by integrating his or her psychological and physical being with spiritual potential.
2. A healthy person has purpose in life. This purpose is reflected in the ability to set immediate and long-range goals that are reflective of his or her life purpose.
3. A healthy person has a sense of self-worth that is well-grounded. Self-worth and self-perception do not change based on material acquisition or loss or on the statements, behaviors, and opinions of others.
4. A healthy person has the capacity to display self-sacrificing love. He or she is able to empathize with the needs and hurts of individuals and society at large. He or she is able to take needed action to help others when appropriate.
5. A healthy person has an accurate view of reality that is not distorted by his or her own needs or pressures arising from the environment.

6. A healthy person has strong internal standards that allow him or her to resist undesirable social and environmental pressures. He or she is able to do the right thing when pressured to do otherwise.

7. A healthy person can react appropriately with strength and courage in the face of stress and potential or actual suffering, accepting what is unchangeable.

8. A healthy person has the ability to enjoy himself or herself and is able to derive fun and relaxation out of life.

9. A healthy person has the freedom to be creative and a contributor in his or her work and personal relationships.

10. A healthy person has his or her physical needs, emotions, and thoughts in balance.

11. A healthy person is able to maintain a future orientation unclouded by hurts and emotional injuries from the past. He or she is able to initiate and receive forgiveness.

12. A healthy person seeks to establish deep, satisfying relationships with a few individuals rather than superficial relationships with many people.[187]

How to Find Your Soul Mate

Selecting a marriage partner is the most important marital decision any person will ever make. When this decision is made well, with full regard for its complexity, marriages end up being satisfying a high percentage of the time. But when it is made too quickly, with too little information, even b y well-meaning persons, the marriage will be tested early and may fail.

The following are a few screening dimensions to look for.

Screening Dimensions for Your Soul Mate

1. **Good Character.** Character, as used here, refers to one's integrity; it has to do, primarily, with honesty.

2. **Kindness.** Kindness is the second most important quality to look for in a mate. Although kind people can often maintain their kindness over time without reciprocation from their mate, the truly great marriages are those in which kindness is matched by kindness.

3. **Quality of Self-Conception.** All emotional health begins with a well-developed self-concept. In a marriage, if both persons know themselves well as individuals, even in their deep places, their individual strength will provide a strong foundation for building a life together even under difficult circumstances.

4. **Having Children.** The parenting of children requires a deep and lasting commitment. If one person has a strong desire to be a parent and the other has none, the match will likely be a poor one, however well the other dimensions are harmonized.

5. **Energy.** Marriages tend to be more successful when the energy levels of two partners are similar.

6. **Spirituality.** First, the specific faith of each person should be the same. Furthermore, it is good to attain "belief alignment" on the role of the church, the nature of God, the place of prayer, the function of biblical authority, and in relation to specific theological matters.

7. **Industry.** This dimension has to do with ones orientation towards work. If one person is a "hard worker" and the other is a "shirker," there will likely be feelings of resentment and guilt.

8. **Artistic Passion.** Most people with strong artistic feelings

and interest (play an instrument, write poetry or music, paint or sing) simply must be paired with partners who have some or the same. Otherwise their marriage seldom works.

9. **Sexual Passion.** Interpersonal chemistry is assessable by the individuals involved in a pairing, and only by them. The goal is to match two persons who have relatively similar levels of sexual passion.

10. **Values Orientation.** It is critical for marital partners to have similar values about the essentials of living.

11. **Family Background.** If one or both of the persons has been raised in a dysfunctional family atmosphere, there needs to be adequate evidence that the impact of this emotional atmosphere has been recognized and worked through. Each person needs to ascertain whether their "in-law" relationships will be positive influences, and if not whether they can be managed effectively.

12. **Intellect.** Research indicates the importance of intellectual equality in a marital partnership; the couple needs to be at a similar intellectual level, whatever that level may be.

13. **Appearance.** Most persons are comfortable being matched with partners within the same "grade level" on appearance.

14. **Sense of Humor.** Laughter is highly therapeutic in every intimate relationship, and there is evidence that marriages in which there is little laughter tend to suffer considerably more during trying times.

15. **Ambition.** Research reveals that two well matched partners need to have approximately the same amount of life ambition. When they do, they will have a common quality that will contribute substantially to the harmonizing of their relationship.

16. **Dominance vs. Submissiveness.** If one partner is highly

dominated, a marriage will work better if the other partner is significantly more submissive.

17. **Communication.** Two life partners need to have a similar level of interest and communication with one another and a similar ability to communicate.

18. **Curiosity.** If one partner is "regularly satisfied" with relatively limited information about anything, while the other partner has a pressing "need to know more," this will typically pull them into two different directions.

19. **Obstreperousness.** One quality that can destroy a marriage and that should be looked at for both potential partners, prior to marriage, is the tendency to find fault, attribute blame, to make the other person wrong, and to need to portray oneself as always "right."

Why Happy Families Are Different

In his bestselling book, *7 Habits of Highly Effective Families*, Stephen Covey compares a successful family to an airplane pilot with a flight plan. For the pilot, the flight plan identifies the destination and outlines the path to getting there. But during the course of the flight, wind, rain, turbulence, air traffic, human error, and other factors act upon that plan. Throughout the trip, there are slight deviations from the plan. But barring anything too major, the plane will arrive at its destination. Likewise, happy families love unique "flight plans" that reflect values and principles that enable them to successfully handle problems and reach the desired "destination."[188] Below are seven habits I have discovered that can create highly effective families.

The Seven Habits Reviewed

Habit 1: **Make deposits**. This deposit involves affirmation and physical touch. When families deposit encouraging words such as "good job," "I love you," "you can do anything you set your mind to do," "you handled that well," "thank you." High balances of emotional reserves are being deposited. When mistakes are made in the relationship there are enough reserves to keep on going.

Habit 2: **Begin with an eternal perspective**. This involves creating a clear vision of what you and your family value. Habit 2 is about "destination" realizing that heaven is our final home with our eternal father. Having a mission statement helps to identify the principles that will keep you focused. Here is one example: Our family mission

- To love God with all of our heart, soul, mind, and strength

- To love each other unconditionally
- To be honest and open with each other
- To always be kind and respectful to one another
- To be committed to our promises
- To keep a feeling of God's presence in the home

Habit 3: **Make prayer a priority.** This habit involves one or both the husband and wife, rising early in the morning before dawn to bow in prayer, and to read the Bible before the day begins. The power of prayer can change the tide of life's daily disturbances and build a strong fortress against the enemy's arrows.

Habit 4: **Consider others.** Think in terms of "we" instead of "me" in order to make family decisions. Happy families think "we" fostering mutual respect and support.

Habit 5: **Listen.** Seek to understand rather than to be understood. Listen carefully and with the intent of understanding the family member's desires, it is then that family members are free to communicate their own thoughts and feelings. Successful families build deep relationships of love and trust by providing helpful feedback.

Habit 6: **Team support.** Two or more people working together can produce more than they can alone. In other words, when each family member contributes to the problem solving, the family is able to accomplish far more in the long run.

Habit 7: **Raising the flag.** Traditions play a significant role in the renewal of family spirit in four basic areas of life: (1) spiritual, (2) mental, (3) emotional, and (4) physical/social. We would do well to realize that a family increases its effectiveness through personal renewal.

Other positive characteristics of healthy families include good communication skills, support and affirmation of family members, respect, trust, family interaction, sense of shared responsibility, abundance of rituals and traditions, and a shared faith in Christ.

Happy families are our greatest natural resource. It is in them that we find our meaning, our strength, and our future.

We've just discovered the elements that make up a happy family. But in order to achieve this goal, we must first look at the beginning of relationships. As Christian believers, the Word of God tells us not to be unequally yoked with unbelievers (2 Corinthians 6:14). Many individuals go into relationships, hoping for the best, but the notion of following a biblical example is very rare in today's world. It's easier to follow the world's view of dating. The world's kind of dating requires no accountability.

We will now look at a biblical relationship. We will attempt to present a different viewpoint of dating by looking at a "courtship model."

What Does a Biblical Relationship Look Like?

Given the biblical theology of sex and marriage, what does a healthy, biblical dating or courting relationship look like in practice?

The attempt to answer that question has brought about a literary flood over the last several years, with different works bearing different levels of usefulness. A few examples include: *Boundaries in Dating*; *Boy Meets Girl*; *I Kissed Dating Goodbye*; *I Hugged Dating Hello*; *I Gave Dating a Chance*; *Her Hand in Marriage*; *The Rules: Time-Tested Secrets for Capturing the Heart of Mr. Right*; and *Wandering Toward the Altar*.

People's responses to these dating styles can be divided into two groups. One group generally supports the method of dating and attempts to instruct readers to date in a "Christian" way. The other group rejects the current dating method altogether as biblically flawed. It advocates an alternative system, which is most often described as *courtship*.

What is the difference between courtship and dating, and is one more biblical than the other? I will provide a working definition of each, describe how the two methods are broadly different, and then recommend why one method is fundamentally more biblical than the other.[189]

Defining Courtship and Dating

Let's begin by defining *courtship*. Courtship ordinarily begins when a single man approaches a single woman by way of the woman's father. He then conducts his relationship with the woman under the authority of her father, family, or church, whichever is most appropriate. Courtship always has marriage as its direct goal.

What, then, is *dating*? Dating, a more modern approach, begins when either the man or the woman initiates a more-than-friends relationship with the other. Then they conduct that relationship outside of any oversight or authority. Dating may or may not have marriage as its goal.

The Differences between Courtship and Dating

What are the differences between these two systems? For our purposes, there are three broad differences between what has been called biblical courtship and modern dating.

The Difference in Motive

The first difference lies with the man's motive in pursuing the relationship. Biblical courtship has one motive—to find a spouse. A man will court a particular woman because he believes it is possible that he could marry her, and courtship is the process of discerning whether that belief is correct. To the extent that the Bible addresses premarital relationships at all, it uses the language of men marrying and women being given in marriage (Matthew 24:38; Luke 20:34–35).

Numbers 30:3–16 talks about a transfer of authority from the father to the husband when a woman leaves her father's house and is united to her husband. The Song of Solomon showcases the meeting, courtship, and marriage of a couple—always with marriage in view. I am not advocating arranged marriages. Rather, I am pointing toward the biblical purpose for young men and women associating with one another. These passages do not argue that marriage should be the direct goal of such relationships so much as they assume it.

Modern dating, on the other hand, need not have marriage as a goal at all. Dating can be recreational. Not only is "dating for fun" acceptable, it is assumed that "practice" and learning by "trial and error" are necessary, and even advisable, before finding the person that is just right for you. The fact that individuals will be emotionally—and probably physically—intimate with many people before settling down with the "right person" is just part of the deal.

However, there is no biblical support for such an approach to marriage. How many examples of "recreational dating" do we see among God's people in the Bible? Zero. The category of premarital intimacy does not exist, other than in the context of grievous sexual sin.

The biblical motive for dating or courting is **marriage.**

The Difference in Mind-Set

The second major difference between biblical courtship and modern dating is the mind-set couples have when interacting with one another. "How do I know if I've found the one?" And what is the unspoken ending to that question? "For me." Will this person make *me* happy? Will this relationship meet *my* needs? How does she look? What is the chemistry like? Have I done as well as I can do?

Selfishness is not what drives a biblical marriage and therefore should not be what drives a biblical courtship. Biblical courtship recognizes the general call to "do nothing out of selfish ambition or vain conceit, but in humility consider others better than yourselves" (Philippians 2:3 NIV). It also recognizes the specific call that Ephesians 5:25 gives to men in marriage, where their main role is one of sacrificial service. Men are to love our wives as Christ loved the church, giving himself up for her. That means loving sacrificially every day. Biblical courtship means that a man does not look for a laundry list of characteristics that comprise his fantasy woman so that his every desire can be fulfilled. Instead he looks for a godly woman as Scripture defines her—a woman he can love and, yes, be attracted to, but also a woman he can serve and love as a godly husband.

In other words, modern dating asks, "How can I find the one for me?," while biblical courtship asks, "How can I be the one for her?"

The Difference in Methods

Most practically, modern dating and biblical courtship are different in their methods. And this is where the rubber really meets the road. In modern dating, intimacy precedes commitment. In biblical courtship, commitment precedes intimacy.

According to the current school of thought, the best way to figure out whether you want to marry a particular person is to act as if you are married and see if you like it. Spend large amounts of time alone together. Become each other's primary emotional confidantes. Share your deepest secrets and desires. Get to know that person better than anyone else in your life. Grow your physical intimacy and intensity on the same track as your emotional intimacy. What you do and say together is private and is no one else's business, and since the relationship is private, you need not submit to anyone else's authority or be accountable. And if this pseudo-marriage works for both of you, then get married. But if one or both of you do not like how it is going, go ahead and break up, even if it means going through something like an emotional—and probably physical—divorce.

Such is the process of finding "the one," and this can happen with several different people before one finally marries. In the self-centered world of secular dating, we want as much information as possible to ensure that the right decision is being made, and if we can enjoy a little physical or emotional comfort along the way, great.

Clearly, this is not the biblical picture. The process just described is hurtful to the woman that the man purports to care about, not to mention himself. And it clearly violates the command of 1 Thessalonians 4:6 not to wrong or defraud our sisters in Christ by implying a marriage-level commitment where one does not exist. It will have a damaging effect on the man's marriage and hers, whether they marry each other or not.

In a biblical relationship, commitment precedes intimacy. Within this model, the man should follow the admonition in 1 Timothy 5:1–2 to treat all young women to whom he is not married as sisters, with absolute purity. The man should show leadership and willingness to bear the risk of rejection by defining the nature and the pace of the relationship. He should do this before spending significant time alone with her in order to avoid hurting or confusing her.

He should also seek to ensure that a significant amount of time is spent with other couples or friends rather than alone. The topics, manner, and frequency of conversations should be characterized by the desire to become acquainted with each other more deeply but not in a way that defrauds each other. There should be no physical intimacy outside the context of marriage, and the couple should seek accountability for the spiritual health and progress of the relationship, as well as for their physical and emotional intimacy.

Within this model, both parties should seek to find out, before God, whether they should be married, and whether they can serve and honor God better together than apart. The man should take care not to treat any woman like his wife if she is not his wife. Of course, he must get to know his courting partner well enough to make a decision on marriage. However, prior to the decision to marry, he should always engage with her emotionally in a way he would be happy for other men to engage her.

In all these ways, a biblical relationship looks different from a secular relationship. If this is done well, God will be glorified.

Now that you know the importance of having accountability in dating/courtship, we will move into courtship that involves children. As a parent, dating becomes much more serious, as you will discover in the next chapters.

Dating and Your Children

Okay, here you are now: divorced, scared, ashamed, and doubting if you want to introduce your new partner to your kids. What do you feel now? Most likely you have the same doubts you did before introducing your teenage friend to your parents. This is the main call of this article.[190]

Before somebody steps into your life, you shouldn't doubt whether to invite them in or not. You cannot let your children suffer once again if it appears that this is the wrong person. You cannot let your children experience a loss all over again. Children may ask, "Did I do something wrong?" Think twice, and make your conclusions carefully.

It is a proven fact that children of divorce are the ones who suffer from separation most of all. They suffer all the emotions that adults experience after divorce—multiplied several times.

Your children always need to come first in a dating/courting relationship. They are completely dependent on your wisdom to keep them safe. Keep your dating/courting life separate from your kids until you know if you are going to be good friends or more with the person. It is hard on kids to get close to someone, only to have that person disappear because you broke up. Your children are in a more complicated situation than you are. They need more attention now than ever before. Fragility: that's the name of that tune.

Typical Conditions of Children in Divorced Families

- They may secretly be hoping that Mommy and Daddy will get back together again and will act out ways to accomplish this.

- They may be jealous and possessive of the single parent's love, not wanting to share Mom and/or Dad with anyone else.
- They may be fearful of losing the single parent. "I lost my dad. Is my mom next?"
- They may not trust any outsiders.
- They may be upset by their single parent dating and expressing romantic feelings for someone other than the other parent.

Caring about your children after divorce is not only crucial for them but for you as well. Actually, it is a blessing for you to have someone to love and care for in this particular moment of your life. It helps a lot not to concentrate on your own emotions, and it heals like nothing else. From any point of view—practical, spiritual, or psychological—caring for someone who needs care more than you do heals you much faster and more effectively.

This topic might be endless, and each and every situation should be considered separately.

You are divorced. The person who used to live with you is no longer in the house. But you are not alone. Besides friends and relatives, your children are with you. They look to you. They do not want to feel emptiness, and you do not want that either. Talk to your children and spend as much time with them as you can. Allow them to express their thoughts about the changes that have occurred. Pray with your children. Focus on what's happening now: the fun, school, what happened today. It will help them, and it will help you adjust more easily to this new life.

Guidelines for Helping Children through Divorce

- Never say bad things about your former spouse to your child, even if your "ex" was not a healthy person. Your child has a right to love and forgive. Don't take away this right. The other parent will stay father or mother for your child forever. Don't cause a trauma to your child by leading him to think that he is a child of garbage.

- Do not think that a small child is different from a teenager in accepting your new partner. Kids mostly feel but do not analyze. And this feeling is impossible to deceive. If your five-year-old does not like your choice, it is hardly possible that he will change his attitude at fourteen—unless your new partner changes himself. This is very rare, but sometimes it happens.

- Before you start dating again, try to "socialize" your child. Spend more time with friends, in good company, so that when you start dating, your children won't feel that your date is taking away their time with you. It will just be a normal time going out.

- Let your children know that their relationship with you will not change because you are beginning to court. When your children are secure and assured in their relationship with you, they are less likely to feel afraid.

- Spend as much time with your kids as you can. Spend this time both by yourself and with your potential spouse. It will tell your children that they are important and that you are paying attention to their needs.

- Listen to your kids. Let them express their thoughts and impressions of your new date. It is not only good for them to feel important to you, but you can also find out some very interesting things about your new partner. A child's view is free from "adult wisdom," and they see things as they are. This can be very helpful.

- Do not criticize your children in the presence of your new partner. And don't allow your date to discipline your kids. Otherwise kids will realize that somebody more important has come into your life. They will not feel secure.

- Don't introduce casual dating partners to your children. Children become attached easily and then suffer more loss. Having a revolving door with many short-term relationships in your child's life causes ambivalence. Consider which model your children will follow when they grow up.

- Do not force an introduction of your new date. If you have already decided they are the right person, do not force your children to meet or accept them. Give them time to get to know the new person in your life. If handled correctly and given time, your child will accept the relationship.

Being divorced with children is often challenging and exhausting. There are two schools of thought. One school says to wait until the children become adults—at least eighteen years old or out of high school—before dating/courting again. This school of thought has in mind the protection of the children and focuses on a secure, emotionally stable family structure.

The second school of thought says it is not fair to torture the divorced parent who has sexual needs or the children who need both a father and mother in the home. The caveat is not to become desperate. Too many women become afraid that they will never be loved, that they will never be provided for financially and will live in poverty. They may believe the false notion that God is not with them. This can be overwhelming for the divorcee.

But this is far from the truth. God is always with us. He is a present help in time of trouble. Therefore, you need to guard against becoming anxious. As a rule of thumb, you should not invite someone to meet your children until at least four months after you begin dating. This will allow you to see whether or not you like the prospective partner before introducing them to your children.

It is sometimes difficult to balance parenting and courting at the same time. Don't forget that communication with your child is always the goal, no matter the situation. When it comes to protecting children, it is a matter to be taken very seriously.

We will now discuss the profile of a pedophile. Hopefully, this information will help you to look for signs that may tell you whether or not the individual you are dating is psychologically healthy.

Profile of a Pedophile

How do pedophiles work? How do they get children to agree to be sexual with them? What is their *modus operandi*? I will attempt to give you an overview of the way pedophiles operate and how parents can take steps to protect their kids.[191]

First we shall define our terms. There is a difference between a child molester and a pedophile. A child molester is one who targets a child he sees and acts on his impulse. He will grab the child, perform sexual acts, and then sometimes murder the child. This is the criminal who will snatch a child from the grocery store, the mall, the park, or even from in front of the child's own house. While child molesters are often strangers, they can also be family members, neighbors, or friends of the family.

Many pedophiles, on the other hand, genuinely like kids. Somewhere along the way, their thinking regarding love, sex, and kids becomes completely muddled. Many of them are very insecure and lonely. They feel that only children will give them unconditional love, and in their psychologically unbalanced minds, they equate love with sex, even when the object of their affection is a child. They do not view their behavior as wrong. They believe that adult men have the right to have sex with kids if there is "mutual consent." They feel that they are far in advance of the viewpoints of society on this issue.

A high percentage of pedophiles had bad experiences during their childhoods. Some were sexually abused themselves. Many lacked a good male role model. Some were actually abused by their fathers or had fathers who withheld love from them. This made them feel unworthy, insecure, lonely, and without love. They reason that if their own fathers could not love them, they must be worthless creatures indeed. Or their thinking has gone the other way, and they decide that their fathers did love them and that abuse must be a way of showing love. Their thinking has become warped, their psyches deeply wounded. An important part of the pedophile never grew up but remained a hurt child.

Many pedophiles do childlike things. They still color in coloring books, play in the sandbox with their little trucks, and decorate their rooms with toys and items that reflect the age of the child they are fixated with. They say things like, "I see the world through the eyes of a child" or "Growing old is mandatory; growing up is optional." They read children's books, see kid-oriented movies, and play children's games. They think of themselves as kids and are much more comfortable around kids than around other adults.

Pedophiles find ways to be around children as often as possible. They get jobs as teachers, camp counselors, school bus drivers, daycare workers, or even enter the priesthood. They volunteer as Boy Scout leaders, church or secular youth workers. Of course most of the people in these professions and volunteer positions are *not* pedophiles and are indeed honest, moral, and upright people, but most pedophiles will seek out these types of occupations and volunteer positions. They look for opportunities to be around kids as much as possible.

Some will even marry or become roommates with women who have children. Or they become friends with single moms in order to have access to their kids. They seek out those kids whose fathers are no longer in their lives. The moms usually see these men as an answer to their prayers, for here at last is a man who is willing to spend time with their children and be that role model they've been looking for. Kids crave attention, affection, and kindness, and here is someone who is willing to give these things to their child. Little do they know that this man they trust, who comes across as being friendly, helpful, and trustworthy is a pedophile and is quite knowledgeable about the methods of child seduction.

Pre-Abuse Grooming

The first stage in child sexual abuse can be a series of subtle behaviors and statements that are often referred to as *grooming*.

Generally, sexual abuse does not occur at random but is a result of the selection of certain children for grooming in the role of victim. Grooming, which can take many forms, is an insidious and malignant process of child seduction, leading to sexual exploitation and abuse.

Initially, in the induction or pre-recruitment stage, the child may be flattered by the attention of the adult and may respond to the preferential treatment they receive from the perpetrator. Children most at-risk for grooming are children who have experienced a significant degree of emotional, social, or economic disadvantage.

Generally, some form of relationship between the victim and perpetrator is established prior to the initiation of sexual advances. The sexual initiation phase is a key turning point in the relationship between the adult and the child, and its significance is rarely acknowledged by the child, whose response may range from complete denial and emotional paralysis, on the one hand, to outright protest and rejection on the other. Unfortunately, the former is the more usual response, and perpetrators typically gamble on the likelihood that the relationship between them and the children, e.g., father/daughter, immobilizes the child's natural defense system.

Experienced perpetrators have an uncanny knack for predicting just how far their actions can proceed before alienating a child victim. Grooming is complete when the relationship progresses to a stage of entrapment where the children experiences themselves as having no choice but to participate in the sexual act.

Common Tactics of Sexual Abusers

- Paying attention to a child who appears emotionally needy
- "Accidentally" or purposefully exposing himself (coming out of the bath, wearing shorts that allow a view of the genitals, openly praising nudity as "normal," etc.)
- Giving gifts or money, taking the child places, providing alcohol or drugs
- Bringing himself down to the child's level of play (becoming the child's buddy)
- Physical contact such as wrestling, tickling, pats on the butt, etc.
- Showing adult magazines or films, letting the child know that he or she can come to them for sexual information or concerns
- Telling the child that he needs to examine the child's body for some reason
- Asking intrusive questions about the child's sexual development, fantasies, or masturbation habits, or giving the child more information about sex than is appropriate for the child's age or development level
- Staring at the child or looking at his or her body in a way that makes the child uncomfortable

A pedophile will spend a lot of time getting the child ready for seduction. Sometimes he will take months or even a year or two, grooming and preparing the child. He uses this time to build up the child's trust in him and to get the child to see him as his best friend. He slowly seduces the child by doing such things as playing with him and being in close contact with him. He will tickle the child and give him "tummy farts." He will watch movies with the child and sit very close to him, often putting his arm around the child or even having the child sit on his lap. The child, of course, feels that this man really cares about him and that he can talk to him about anything.

If a father figure or other male role model is missing from the child's life, then of course the pedophile knows that this child is just the victim he is looking for. He, however, does not view the child as a victim but as a person he can share love, fun, and pleasure with. The thing to remember is that the pedophile does not think like a normal adult. Indeed, he has serious psychological imbalances and views his actions in the same way as an adult male who is attempting seduction of an adult female. And the pedophile does not usually stop with just one child. He often grooms several at once. Sometimes he is grooming some while actually in the sexual relationship stage with others.

A pedophile will take the child he is grooming many places, such as to movies, roller skating rinks, amusement parks, the zoo, fairs, and festivals. He spends a lot of time with the child and invests as much money as possible. He buys the child toys and even gives him clothes and trinkets. He spends as much time alone with the child as he can. What child would not have warm feelings toward a man who acts like he truly cares about him, pays him a lot of attention, and spends an enormous amount of time and money on him? Most pedophiles are likable people, and they groom the kids to like them.

A pedophile may have a group of children he seduces at the same time. Sometimes he will invite the neighborhood children to his home to watch videos and play video games. He will give them candy and other snack foods. Eventually he will bring out the video camera. Often the kids are groomed for months before he builds up their trust enough to let him fondle them and use the video camera on them. This is one of the ways that child pornography makes its rounds on nasty Internet sites.

The pedophile loves it when the child has his own e-mail address. This way, he can correspond with the child whenever he wishes and say things that will make the grooming process go even faster.

Many pedophiles are becoming quite adept at finding their victims online. They use screen names that are attached to profiles describing themselves as young teens. Then they go into kid and teen chat rooms looking for kids they think may be easy prey. If they happen to get caught doing this, they will say that they only go in these rooms to feel like a kid again and to relieve the stresses of life. They will swear that they never went into a private chat with any child. If you believe that, I have oceanfront property in Arizona I could sell you. The truth is that not only do they go into private chats with some of the kids, they often take it a step further and set up times and places to meet a few young teens in person.

The pedophile will tell the child such things as, "How would your mother feel if she knew you and I had done this? You started it, you know. You came on to me. It would be just terrible on her, and she might even commit suicide or something." He tries to make the child feel guilty, ashamed, and afraid so he won't tell anyone.

Most friends, relatives, neighbors, coworkers, and acquaintances are shocked when they find out that the man they know and like so much is a pedophile. They would never have guessed it, as he always seemed so likable, helpful, and friendly.

Some pedophiles prefer sexual relations with other men over sex with women, but the main focus of their desire is young boys who are around the age of puberty. Most pedophiles have never been able to maintain a close and loving sexual relationship with either men or women.

How do you know if your child has already been seduced or molested or approached by a pedophile? There are warning signs to look for. If your child has always liked school but suddenly does not want to go, something is going on. It could be that he has merely had a fight with another student or was scolded by a teacher. On the other hand, perhaps someone has approached him in a sexual way. Is there a change in his behavior, or have his grades taken a nosedive? If so, it's time to take a look at what may be going on in the child's life that you don't know about. The same holds true if your child suddenly has mood changes or aggressive behavior that he did not previously display.

Does your child suddenly seem withdrawn and preoccupied? Does he have new toys, clothes, or money that you can't account for? Does he have a loss of appetite? Does he have nightmares or trouble sleeping at night? Does he exhibit sexual behavior or language that is inappropriate for his age? Does he draw pictures of the private parts of the human body? All of these things are signs that it's time to find out what's going on. If you don't feel comfortable talking to your child about these things, then find someone who does. Don't be afraid or ashamed to take your child to counseling if you are concerned that someone may have harmed or tried to harm him. If you don't help him in this way, who will?

Eleven Ways to Spot a Pedophile

The first thing to remember is that pedophiles are master communicators. They are very good at sliding into a family and befriending the parents to gain access to their kids. But there are warning signs that may indicate that someone has less-than-honest intentions with your family.[192]

Preferential child molesters and pedophiles have distinct patterns of behavior that are highly predictable. As a parent, it is crucial that you learn to identify these patterns as warning signs, as they are an extremely valuable tool in assessing whether someone represents a risk to your children.

Each one of these characteristics, taken on their own, may mean little. But if you can identify a large number of them in an individual you know, you need to remove that person from your child's environment and never allow him to have unsupervised access.

A pedophile could be someone who:

1. Shows an intense interest in children and childlike things. It is hard not to care about kids. In fact, you may be suspicious of those who show no interest in children at all. However, there is a balance between average or appropriate interest, and excessive interest. Pedophiles will find everything about your child interesting, seem to relate to them better than adults, and prefer their company.

2. Has idealistic views of children. A pedophile may refer to children as "pure" and "innocent" and put them on a pedestal. They may think of children as "projects," offering them extra help after school, for instance, or arranging meetings with the child for ostensibly good and honest reasons. They will sometimes invest a great deal of time and effort in one child, rather than offering equal attention to an entire group of kids. Some pedophiles have a belief that they are looking out for and have genuine love for children.

3. Has limited peer relationships. A pedophile feels more comfortable around children. They do not often associate with peers in their age group. They would much prefer to sit at the "children's table" at a dinner party than with the adults.

4. Calls children "friends." Pedophiles will surround themselves with childlike things that attract children and encourage friendships. A pedophile will often be the "cool older guy" in town, and you may find that many kids hang out at his house. He will attract kids with his lack of rules and defiance of parental rules and controls.

5. Is over twenty-five years old, single, never married, and lives alone or with parents. Just because someone matches this description does not mean he is a pedophile. However, if he meets several other criteria listed here, you should see this as a warning sign.

6. Moves often and unexpectedly. Often pedophiles will feel they have "worn out their welcome" in a particular community or feel that they are close to getting caught. They will move regularly to avoid detection or confrontation from suspecting parents, or to find a new pool of victims.

7. Participates and organizes activities that exclude other adults. For obvious reasons, a pedophile needs access and privacy to commit the abuse. He will avoid inviting other adults on planned events or outings.

8. Takes excessive photographs of children. Pedophiles collect photographs, mementos, symbols, and anything else from their victims and or other targets that might enhance their fantasies. Most notably, they take an inappropriate number of pictures or videos of children in their communities, at events, or simply when playing. The pedophile may also have a lot of child-focused movies or music CDs, more than seems appropriate for a single man to possess. These are used for fantasy as well as to lure children into their homes.

9. Works and plays in areas that attract children. Pedophiles typically choose work environments that allow access to children. This may include working in a school (as a teacher or in some other capacity) or daycare, as a coach, as a volunteer in a community center, or in any other profession that is child-focused.

10. Decorates his home with childlike décor. A pedophile is constantly trying to attract children, and he relates to them better than to adults. His home, dress, and demeanor will often reflect childlike characteristics.

11. Is generous with gifts. Many pedophiles choose targets that are needy—both for material things and for attention. They are quick to provide a needy child with toys, games, and money to lure them into a position of trust and eventually a sense of indebtedness.

Parents, not the kids, are the ones who decide who comes into the kids' lives. Always pay close attention to people who associate with your kids. If you have a bad feeling about one of them, or your child expresses discomfort, listen.

Although we have extensively discussed the importance of protecting your children from potential abusers, it is important to know that there are healthy people still in the world today, individuals who, like you, want to develop a successful family life. In the next chapter, we will look at the subject of blended families and discover tools that can help.

Blended Families

More than half of all Americans live in some sort of nontraditional family as a result of remarriage. While it can be a rocky road, not all blended families necessarily resemble Cinderella's. Merge yours, mine, and ours with as few bumps as possible by recognizing how stepfamilies differ from nuclear ones—and by having lots and lots of healthy communication.[193]

At Home

1. Give each child personal, private space. This includes a *bed*, *drawers*, *closet space*, a *desk*, and a *chair* at the dinner table. This is especially important for nonresident kids.
2. Create a master family calendar that shows who, where, and when. Mark special events for both resident and nonresident kids. Coordinate the family calendar together.
3. Arrange a signed consent form that allows the stepparent to authorize emergency medical treatment for all the children.
4. Start with a clean slate. To resolve turf wars, it's often easier to just sell the old house and move to one that's new to everyone.
5. Use stepfamily support networks, a licensed social worker, or your church or synagogue to find positive solutions to problems as they come up.

Communication

6. Take classes on stepparenting before the merger. Type

"stepparenting resources" or "blended families" into a search engine or contact a child care referral service in your area.

7. Hold regular family meetings to discuss issues as they come up, and work out each week's logistics. The structure will be helpful to all kids.

8. Talk to your spouse about the best way to handle disciplining each other's kids. Ideally, you'll parent as a team and be firmly in the same camp when it comes to establishing ground rules, setting limits, and defining what's appropriate. When discussing your spouse's child—or any child—criticize the *behavior*, not the *child*.

Part-Time Kids, Full-Time Kids

9. Accept the fact that a blended family will not act or feel like your picture of an "ideal" family. The part-time kids can get jealous of the full-time kids and feel left out. Don't rush to try to create a harmonious family feeling. Be patient and prayerful—and creative.

10. Foster an atmosphere of open communication, and talk about issues when they come up. Strike a balance between having everyone's feelings heard and doing what needs to be done. Keep it simple, and talk to each child at his or her own level.

11. Set up rules and expectations regarding behavior and schedules, and enforce them consistently. Your part-time kids may have different rules in their other home, but it's helpful all around when everyone knows what to expect at your house. Insist that everyone speak to and treat one another with respect.

Relationships

12. Plan regular private talks about family issues. Discuss with your new spouse what your mutual long-term goals are. What do you want your part-time kids to remember from growing up in their new family (since it won't be about routine and consistency). Talk about what type of family structure and activities you can both put in place to support those long-term goals.

13. Let kids and stepparents work out differences without your help. They need to learn how to work together within the guidelines you set—and biological parents need to stay out of the middle.

14. Make sure *every* child feels wanted in your home, whether he or she lives there full-time, half-time, or just two weekends a month.

15. Be sure biological family members have some one-on-one time each week, especially at first. At the same time, plan time with your new stepchildren. Kids are often less dramatic if there's no audience to play to.

16. Talk to each other. Tell lots of stories and look at photo albums. Create rituals for this new configuration. Listen to the kids, and slowly, patiently develop a common history with them as you grow into a new family.

17. Be as patient as possible, no matter how difficult a phase your new family is in. Don't expect overnight success: It typically takes two to five years for a newly blended family to stabilize.

The Ex

18. Maintain a civil relationship with your ex and your spouse's ex. Never bad-mouth the other parent in front of the children.
19. Communicate with the other parent when solving any ongoing problem a child might have. Operating as a team is absolutely in your child's best interests.
20. Establish a visitation schedule and stick to it as much as possible. Don't let your child make plans for days when he or she is supposed to be with Dad or Mom. Inform the ex as far in advance as possible if you do need to change the schedule.

Tips and Warnings

- Give each child a caddy for grooming supplies when they share a bathroom.
- Make holiday plans far in advance.
- Make—and keep—a weekly date night with your spouse. Plan an overnight getaway with your spouse.
- The stepparent would be wise to follow the biological parent's lead on disciplining style, and when it's possible, leave the disciplining up to him or her.
- Let your children take their time when they are deciding what to call the new stepparent. Start at a neutral, conservative place, such as the parent's first name. They can always move to a more intimate name like "Papa [first name]"—or even "Dad"—as their relationship and sense of comfort and security develops over time.
- During the beginning stages of a relationship, plan trips and adventures with all the kids on neutral ground.

- Recognize common stepfamily traps, such as jealousy and resentment, when they arise, and try not to take them personally.
- As much as possible, go as a couple to pick up the children. This helps each individual to see what the new norm is.

Blended Families: Merging Two Families under One Roof

The God we serve is the wonderful God of second chances. Once you have identified a marriage partner that is healthy for you and your children, it's important that you both discover how to blend a family. Due to the fact that it is not a nuclear family (children from the same biological mother and father), blended families require much more intentional structuring than nuclear families. In the next pages, we will discover the challenges and the joys of bringing together a blended family. God places the lonely into families.

Parenting your own children is difficult enough, even under the best of circumstances. However, trying to raise the children of your spouse from a previous marriage or relationship is a trial-by-error task at best. With more and more marriages ending in divorce, the blended family is quickly becoming a common trend. Statistics report that the number of blended families is growing each year, not shrinking. In fact, the blended family has become the most common form of family.

The most difficult challenge many of these blended families face is trying to function as a single-family unit. In a blended family, everything from holidays to bedtime and daily routines must sometimes be decided at a moment's notice. Different family histories, traditions, memories, and sometimes even different cultures must be taken into account.

Another obstacle blended families face is favoritism or loyalty conflicts. Although considered normal, this can be stressful for everyone. Parents may find themselves torn between filling the needs of their spouse, their children, or even their ex. More often than not, the biological parent feels caught between his or her spouse and one or more of the children regarding rules, discipline, and fairness. Even if all parents agree that a stepparent has the authority to discipline stepchildren, the children may not agree, causing them to resist, act out, or get depressed. Just as with biological families, if the kids sense any tension between the parents, especially regarding discipline or rules, they will exploit the opportunity in order to gain power over the other children or stepparent.

Before jumping into a blended family situation, take heed as to how well you and your spouse solve problems together. This is going to become a huge factor in the overall success of your blended family life.

Blended families are on the rise. These relationships can be difficult, but with time and a lot of patience, two families can successfully become one.[194]

Discipline in the Blended Family

People frequently ask me if their disciplinary methods should be different in a blended family.[195]

Your kids have been through the separation of their parents, and then a divorce, and now a new marriage that comes with a blended family. You wonder, shouldn't I just give my kids a break and loosen up on my discipline?

Top Reasons for Your Discipline to Remain the Same

- Your values haven't changed, and you should continue to teach your children the difference between right and wrong.
- Boundaries and guidelines show your children that you love them.
- Providing discipline actually gives the consistency and security your kids need at a time when a lot of things are changing around them.

How to Handle the Kids

You have remarried, and you need to agree with your new spouse on what discipline is fair to both adults. It's important to respect the biological parent's history of parenting but still come to a mutual understanding of how all children will be treated and disciplined in your home. It's time for the two of you to discuss boundaries and guidelines for your kids and for your home.

All kids should be treated fairly and equally. You and your spouse create house rules such as:

- No eating in the living room
- No TV after nine p.m. on a school night
- Everyone helps clean up the kitchen after meals

These rules will apply to every child in your family. Consequences can be different, based on age differences and developmental state, but consequences still need to be equal and fair—allowing a few exceptions when necessary.

Note: It also helps if the adults follow the same rules. It's hard to explain why Dad is eating in the living room when no one else can!

The Biological Parent Takes the Lead

The biological parent should always take the lead in front of the kids. The new stepparent should not be perceived as the "heavy" who enforces or creates the rules.

If your child disobeys a house rule, deal with the issue with your spouse at your side. The children should always see you two as a united front. Even if you don't agree on everything, appear to them to be united, and work out the differences later, in private.

Be Consistent

If you make a rule, keep it every day. Don't change the rules on the days you are tired or the days your spouse is out of the house or out of town.

No Secret Alliances with Your Biological Kids

If you change the rules when your spouse is not there, this causes your children to not respect their stepparent and to believe that their bond with you is stronger than the bond between you and your spouse. *Your relationship with your spouse should take priority.* Keeping a strong relationship with your spouse provides a stable and consistent environment for your children. This stability and consistency will create feelings of security for your children and will move your blended family toward being a strong, successful, united family.

Creating a strong, stable foundation for marriage can help to ensure a lifetime of love and commitment. We have saved the best for last, which is discovering how to begin on a solid footing for marriage. If you are single, engaged, or married, you'll benefit from the next chapter on the best ways to prepare for marriage.

The Worst and Best Ways to Prepare for Marriage [196]

With half of all marriages ending in divorce, millions of couples have decided to begin a trial marriage in which they live with each other to test whether the relationship works. In fact, cohabitation is now the dominant way that seriously dating Americans decide whether to marry.

It is the worst possible preparation for marriage. Yet the US Census Bureau reported in March 1970 that 523,000 unmarried couples were living together. In March 1993 the figure had shot up to 3.5 million couples—a sevenfold increase. Between 2009 and 2010 there was a 13 percent increase, (868,000) in the number of opposite sex couples who were cohabitating.

The University of Wisconsin conducted a national survey of families and households back in 1989 and came to similar conclusions. After interviewing fourteen thousand people in one-hundred-minute personal interviews, reconstructing their sexual and marital histories, the study found the following. According to Dr. Larry Bumpass, the survey's director, "The proportion of first marriages that were preceded by cohabitation increased from 8 percent in the late 1960s to 49 percent among those in 1985–86."

The percentages continue to increase today. In 2009 there were an estimated 6.7 million unmarried couples living together, while in 2010 there were 7.5 million.

What was morally reprehensible for centuries and was derided as "shacking up" is now the accepted norm.

What is the consequence of widespread cohabitation? The result is disaster. In fact, cohabitation is a double "cancer" for marriage. The survey reports that "about 40 percent of cohabiting unions in the United States break up without the couples getting married." The average duration is 1.3 years. Afterward, they suffer from what might be called "premarital divorce."

Yet they rarely learn their lessons. In the next relationship, rather than wait until both are committed to marriage, people live with someone else—and with what result? Cohabitation has become a substitute for marriage. It is thus a cancer at the front end of marriage. People who would have found marriage partners in an earlier generation are ending up in their thirties and forties having never married.

Cohabitation is also a cancer at the center of marriage. The survey reports: "Marriages that are preceded by living together have 50 percent higher disruption (divorce or separation) rates than marriages without premarital cohabitation." Instead of a 50 percent risk of failure, those who live together first have a 75 percent risk of divorce.

Rarely Preached

Further, 1.2 million cohabiting couples have children, making it a major engine of illegitimacy. Another million kids see their parents' divorce each year. Two million children every year are the victims of their parents' selfishness.

In the *American Enterprise* magazine, Karl Zinsmeister wrote: "There is a mountain of scientific evidence showing that when families disintegrate, children often end up with intellectual, physical, and emotional scars that persist for life … We talk about the drug crisis, the education crisis, and the problem of teen pregnancy and juvenile crime. But all these ills tract back predominantly to the source: broken families."

A group of pastors was asked, if they had ever preached a whole sermon on cohabitation. None had. "Have any of you preached a whole sermon on divorce?" Again, none had done so. "And we wonder why there is a problem," we, as ministers of the Gospel are neglecting our duty to preach on these concerns.

Scripture is clear on these matters. Paul wrote to the Corinthians that they were to "flee fornication." And Malachi said that the blessings of some priests will be cursed by God. Why?

"For the lips of a priest ought to preserve knowledge, and from his mouth men should seek instruction—because he is the messenger of the Lord Almighty. But you have turned from the way and by your teaching have caused many to stumble" (Malachi 2:7–8 NIV).

A few verses later Malachi discussed divorce: "You flood the Lord's altar with tears. You weep and wail because he no longer pays attention to your offerings … You ask, 'Why?' It is because the Lord is acting as the witness between you and the wife of your youth, because you have broken faith with her, though she is your partner, the wife of your marriage covenant. Has not the Lord made them one? In the flesh and the spirit they are his. And why one? Because He was seeking godly offspring … 'I hate divorce,' says the Lord God of Israel" (2:13–16).

The Best Way to Prepare for Lifelong Marriage

If cohabitation is the wrong way to prepare for a lifelong marriage, what is the right way? About 200,000 engaged couples are fortunate enough to be in churches that know how to help people achieve two great goals: (1) avoid a bad marriage before it begins, and (2) obtain marriage insurance as an engaged couple.

First, these churches administer a premarital inventory or questionnaire for seriously dating couples and for the engaged. One of the best is called PREPARE (Premarital Personal and Relationship Evaluation). It consists of 125 written statements, which both the man and the woman independently mark as to whether they agree or disagree.

The results are sent to be tabulated by computer. What emerges is a remarkably accurate X-ray of the couple's strengths and weaknesses, which are euphemistically called "growth areas." It can predict with about eighty-percent accuracy which couples will divorce and which couples will have a happy marriage.

Of the 100,000 couples who participate each year, 10,000 actually break their engagements because their scores are so bad.

This is good! Better a broken engagement than a broken marriage. Those who break their engagements have scores that are equal to those who marry and later divorce.

Thus PREPARE helps 10,000 couples a year avoid a bad marriage before it begins. Another 5,000 couples postpone their weddings until they work through the surfacing problems. However, for most of the 90 percent who go on to get married, the premarital inventory not only puts a spotlight on conflicts the couple has to resolve but identifies how each partner contributes to the problem.

A premarital inventory can also be a bridge by which a younger generation taps into the wisdom of an older generation.

One of PREPARE's goals is to teach couples how to resolve conflicts by using "Ten Steps for Resolving Conflicts."

Other Elements of Marriage Insurance

The three most important elements of deciding whether to marry someone are (1) taking a premarital inventory, (2) working with an older, solidly married couple to talk through the issues, and (3) testing how well you work as a couple (using the "Ten Steps"). Anyone who really wants marriage insurance should consider the following additional steps. Each will increase the odds of a lifelong marriage.

1. *Chastity*: If an unmarried couple is living together, it may be wise for a church not to marry them until they move apart and live separately for some months. The church could even ask the engaged to consider signing a covenant to limit their sexual contact to no more than French kissing. Those who marry as virgins have much lower divorce rates than those who are sexually active. "*Eros* pushes out God, if you want God as a third partner of your marriage, you have to play by His rules."

2. *Lectures*: A body of substantive information needs to be covered. We ask knowledgeable lay leaders to give a series of eight lectures involving male/female differences in communication, sex within marriage, resolving financial differences, conflict resolution, and scriptural wisdom in building a lasting marriage.

3. *Workbook*: H. Norman Wright has written an excellent workbook, *Before You Say "I Do,"* which requires couples to look up verses of Scripture on the various issues of marriage. It also requires them to develop a joint budget.

4. *Engaged Encounter*: This is the name of a weekend retreat, which is the best single step a young couple can take to improve their communication skills. Married couples share intimate details of their marriage and then ask the engaged couple to write in a workbook the answers to tough questions like, "What things do I talk about with others more easily than I do with you? What are the things that make me angry with you? What doubts do I have about marrying you?" After writing an answer to each question, the couples exchange notebooks and talk about their answers.

A Final Word

Too many churches are preparing couples for weddings rather than for lifelong marriages. Three-fourths of all couples who marry in America do so in a church. Yet more than 50 percent are ending in divorce or separation. Clearly, most churches are only "blessing machines" or "wedding factories."

However, they can be marriage-savers, places where people can really get a start on building a lifelong marriage.

What God has joined together, let the church help hold together.

Summary

Marriage has been given to mankind as a gift. God designed humans as relational beings. Marriage is the highest of all human relationships. Within the bond of marriage, other human beings are produced. Marriage is a covenant relationship, meaning: a *promise*, a legal agreement where both husbands and wives pledge to love, honor, and cherish each other with the covenant promise of monogamy, which means sexual faithfulness to the spouse alone.

When both parties in the marriage covenant keep this agreement, God blesses the marriage, and much satisfaction, contentment, and love are experienced. This blessed state comes as a result of obedience to God's Word, making 1 Corinthians 13 a pattern.

When marriage breaks down and adultery, fornication, or desertion occurs, God has implemented a painful mercy called divorce, which allows for remarriage—but only to Christian believers.

Dr. J. Vernon McGee once said, "Divorce is not the problem, but marriage." What he meant is that the problem is with us from the onset. If we are not mature individuals, whole in spirit, soul, and body, wanting to give rather than take, we are not ready for marriage. The question is not, "What can my spouse do for me." The real question is: "How can I serve my spouse and encourage his or her well-being."

Conclusion

When we look at the word *covenant*, which is a binding agreement that implies perpetual love and affection, we must understand that the institution of marriage should be viewed as the most sacred union among human relationships.

God created Adam and said in Genesis 2:18,[197] "It is not good for man to be alone. I will create a help meet for him." The words *help meet* imply one who is suitable for another. Certainly Eve was suitable for Adam. Adam asserted that she was now bone of his bone and flesh of his flesh. She was to be called *woman* (Genesis 1:23).[198] God instructed them to be fruitful and multiply and replenish the earth (Genesis 1:28).[199]

God also said of this newly formed union, "Therefore shall a man leave his mother and father and cleave to his wife, and they two shall be one flesh" (Genesis 2:24).[200] The word *cleave* means "to adhere closely, stick, cling to, or remain faithful." When the man leaves his parents and cleaves to his wife, they form a family unit. God intended for this structure to be the foundation of society. Out of this family structure God wanted the man and the woman to take responsibility for each other's welfare by loving the mate above all others.

God intended marriage to be a permanent institution. Matthew 19:6[201] says, "Wherefore they are no more twain, but one flesh. What therefore God hath joined together let not man put asunder." Marriage in its highest state is a union in which security and love can be found. God created a lifelong mate to become bonded to a partner who would share in the joys of life as well as each other's sorrows.

Unfortunately, in our modern society we have developed the attitude that "I don't need anyone" and "I can go it alone"—or the other extreme that says, "I'm entitled to it all. If an extramarital affair occurs, so what." These attitudes are destroying the moral fabric of our society, causing single-parent families, most of which are headed by females with children living at or below the poverty level. Young boys have lost any notion of what it means to respect male leadership, because none exists in the home. This is one of the prevalent pictures of a society who has not chosen to follow God's blueprint for marriage, which is in essence "oneness." Husbands and wives need each other, and children need both their parents.

Marriage teaches us sacrifice, patience, and love. The apostle Paul gives us a beautiful picture of this in Ephesians 5:22–32,[202] where he says to the wives, "Submit yourselves to your own husbands as unto the Lord. For the husband is the head of the wife, even as Christ is the head of the church, and He is the savior of the body. Therefore, as the church is subject unto Christ, so let the wives be to their own husbands in everything."

To the husbands, Paul says, "Husbands, love your wives, even as Christ loved the church, and gave himself for it, that he might sanctify and cleanse it with the washing of water by the word, that he might present it to himself a glorious church, not having spot, or wrinkle or any such thing, but that it should be without blemish. So ought men to love their wives as their own bodies."

Paul wrote that wives should submit themselves to their own husbands in all things and that husbands should love their wives as Christ loved the church, even sacrificing himself for it.

Christ's example is typified. To begin with, Christ is the head of the church, and he loved the church so much that he devoted his life to serving it and finally sacrificing himself for it. We, the church, on the other hand, signify at baptism our desire to submit ourselves to Christ in all things.

The permanent bond and love that Christ has for the church,

signifies the kind of bond that husbands and wives should have for one another. The focal point of the marriage relationship is Christ! "For we are members of his body, of his flesh and of his bones. For this cause shall a man leave his father and mother, and shall be joined unto his wife, and they two shall be one flesh" (Ephesians 5:30–31).[203]

This is a love story to be cherished.

Notes

1. Lion Publishing PLC, *New Concise Bible Dictionary*, Tyndale House, pages 337–338.
2. Dake Publishing, Inc., *Dakes Annotated Reference Bible*, Authorized King James Version Text, Genesis 2:18, page 4.
3. Ibid., Hosea 1:3, pages 1489–1491.
4. Ibid., Genesis 2:18, page 4.
5. Ibid., Genesis 2:24, page 4.
6. Wayne A. Mack, *Strengthening Your Marriage*, R & R Printing, pages 1–3.
7. *Dakes Annotated Reference Bible KJV*, Dake Publishing, Inc., Genesis 2:24, page 4.
8. Ibid., Matthew 19:5, page 36.
9. Ibid., Mark 10:7–8, page 81.
10. Ibid., Ephesians 5:31, page 370.
11. Ibid., Exodus 20:12, page 135.
12. Ibid., Mark 7:9–13, page 74.
13. Ibid., 1 Timothy 5:8, page 411.
14. www.Christianitytoday.com/ct/2009/august/theearlycaseformarriage
15. *Life Application Bible NIV*, Tyndale House Publishing, Genesis 2:18–24, pages 8–9.
16. Ibid., Genesis 24:58–60, page 51.
17. Ibid., Genesis 2:24, page 9.
18. *Exhaustive Concordance of the Bible: Greek Dictionary, Index to New Testament*, Zondervan Publishing, page 3879, 3908.
19. Walter A. Elwell, *Evangelical Dictionary of Theology*, Baker Books, "Covenant," page 276,
20. *Dakes Annotated Reference Bible KJV*, Dake Publishing, Inc., Jeremiah 11:4, page 1281, 24:7; page 1301, 30:22; page 1312, 32:38; page 1317.
21. Ibid., Ezekiel 11:20, page 1376, 14:11; page 1380, 36:28; page 1416, 37:23; page 1418.
22. Ibid., Zechariah 8:8, page 1558.
23. Ibid., 1 Samuel 20:8, page 535.
24. Ibid., Song of Songs 4:9–10, page 1129.
25. Ibid., Song of Songs 4:9–10, page 1129.
26. Ibid., Jeremiah 33:10–11, page 1318.
27. Ibid., Revelation 3:20, page 504.

28. Ibid., Malachi 2:14–15, page 1572.
29. www.Marriagefamilyfoundation.org/consequencesimpactonchildren
30. www.Census.gov/poupulationusbureauofcensus. unmarriedcouplehouseholds
31. D. E. Papalia and S. W. Olds, *Human Development*, 7ᵗʰ edition, Boston: McGraw-Hill, 1988.
32. *Dakes Annotated Reference Bible KJV,* Dake Publishing, Inc.. Matthew 5:32.
33. *Life Application Bible NIV,* Tyndale House Publishing, Matthew 19:6, page 1691.
34. Ibid., Deuteronomy 24:1–4, page 312.
35. Ibid., Romans 7:2–3, page 2039.
36. Ibid., Genesis 1:27, page 7.
37. Ibid., 1 Corinthians 6:18, page 2070.
38. Ibid., Ephesians 5:21–33, page 2139.
39. Ibid., Philippians 2:10, page 2148.
40. Ibid., Ephesians 5:25–30, pages 2139, 2140.
41. Ibid., Ephesians 5:23, 32, page 2139.
42. Ibid., Hebrews 13:4, page 2241.
43. Ibid., Philippians 2:3–5, 8, page 2148.
44. Ibid., Genesis 2:18, page 3.
45. Ibid., Genesis 2:18–25, pages 8–9.
46. Ibid., Genesis 2:18–25, pages 8–9.
47. Ibid., Proverbs 31:10–31, pages 1131–1132.
48. Ibid., Ephesians 5:22–24, 33, page 2139.
49. Ibid., Titus 2:4–5, page 2210.
50. Ibid., I Peter 3:1-6 page 2261
51. Ibid., Ephesians 5:21, page 2139.
52. Ibid., Philippians 2:3–4, page 2148.
53. Ibid., 1 Peter 5:5, page 2265.
54. Ibid., Hebrew 13:17, page 2242.
55. Ibid., Proverbs 31:10–31, pages 1131–1132.
56. Ibid., Proverbs 31:26, page 1132.
57. Ibid., Acts 18:26, page 1999.
58. Ibid., Judges 13:21–23, page 406.
59. Ibid., Luke 2:51, page 1794.
60. Ibid., John 5:30, page 1884.
61. Ibid., Ephesians 5:22, page 2139.
62. Ibid., Acts 5:28–29, page 1954.
63. Ibid., Genesis 2:18–22, page 8–9.

64. Ibid., Proverbs 31:12, page 1132.
65. Ibid., 1 Peter 3:1–2, 7, page 2261.
66. Ibid., 1 Peter 3:3–5, page 2261.
67. Ibid., Philippians 4:4, page 2153.
68. Ibid., Proverbs 31:11–12, page 1132.
69. Ibid., Ephesians 4:25, page 2138.
70. Ibid., Philippians 2:3–4, page 2148.
71. Ibid., Ephesians 4:2, 31–32, pages 2137–2138.
72. Ibid., Hebrew 13:5, 16, pages 2241–2242.
73. Ibid., Psalms 128:3, page 1049.
74. Ibid., Proverbs 31:10–31, pages 1131–1132.
75. Ibid., Ephesians 1:7, page 2130.
76. Ibid., 1 John 1:9, page 2276.
77. Ibid., Galatians 5:16, 22–23, pages 2124–2125.
78. Ibid., Philippians 2:12–13, page 2149.
79. Ibid., Ephesians 5:22, page 2139.
80. Ibid., Ephesians 5:25–33, page 2139.
81. Ibid., Ephesians 5:25–33, page 2139.
82. Ibid., Genesis 3:16, page 12.
83. Ibid., Ephesians 5:23–33, page 2139.
84. Ibid., 1 Timothy 3:4–5, page 2191.
85. Ibid., Psalms 128, page 1049.
86. Ibid., 1 Peter 3:7, page 2261.
87. Ibid., 1 Corinthians 7:3–4, page 2071.
88. Ibid., Proverbs 5:15–19, pages 1080–1081.
89. Ibid., Colossians 3:19, page 2166.
90. Ibid., Ephesians 5:23, page 2139.
91. Ibid., 1 Timothy 3:4–5, 12, page 2191.
92. Ibid., 1 Corinthians 11:3, page 2081.
93. Ibid., Matthew 20:20–28, pages 1694–1695.
94. Ibid., John 13:1–15, page 1908.
95. *Dakes Annotated Reference Bible KJV*, Dake Publishing, Inc., Philippians 2:6–8, page 378.
96. Ibid., Ephesians 5:23–33, page 378.
97. Ibid., John 1:39, 43, page 164.
98. Ibid., Mark 1:17; 3:14; 4:10, 5:1, 30–31, 40; 6:1, pages 62–71.
99. Ibid., Matthew 5:2, page 6.
100. Ibid., 1 Peter 3:7, page 468
101. Ibid., Mark 1:35, page 63.
102. Ibid., 1 John 2:1, page 481.

103. Ibid., John 4:1–2, page 168.
104. Ibid., Mark 1:35–39, page 63.
105. Ibid., John 11:39–44, pages 188–189.
106. Ibid., Matthew 10:1–14, pages 16–17.
107. Ibid., Romans 5:8, page 286.
108. Ibid., Ephesians 1:6–7, page 364.
109. Ibid., John 13:1b, page 193.
110. Ibid., Jeremiah 31:3b, page 1312.
111. Ibid., Philippians 2:6–7, page 378.
112. Ibid., Ephesians 5:26–27, page 370.
113. Ibid., Ephesians 5:2, 25, pages 369–370.
114. Ibid., Galatians 2:20, page 355.
115. Ibid., 1 Peter 3:18, page 468.
116. Ibid., Romans 5:6–11, page 286.
117. Ibid., 1 Peter 2:24, page 467.
118. Ibid., John 10:1–14, page 185–186.
119. Ibid., John 14:1–3, page 195.
120. Ibid., John 13:34–35, page 194.
121. Ibid., John 15:9–10, page 197.
122. Ibid., Romans 8:32, page 292.
123. Ibid., Philippians 4:13, 19, page 381.
124. Ibid., Hebrews 4:14–16, page 433.
125. Ibid., 1 Peter 3:7, page 468.
126. Ibid., Ephesians 5:28, page 370.
127. Ibid., 1 John 1:9, page 481.
128. Ibid., Matthew 5:23–24, page 7.
129. Ibid., James 5:16, page 461.
130. Ibid., Ephesians 1:7, page 364.
131. Ibid., Luke 11:13, page 126.
132. Ibid., Galatians 5:16, 22, 23, pages 359–360.
133. Ibid., Philippians 2:12–13, page 378.
134. Ibid., James 1:19–24, page 456.
135. *Life Application Bible*, Tyndale House, Colossians 4:6 NIV, Zondervan Publishing, 1991.
136. Ibid., 1 Corinthians 7:2–5, page 2071.
137. *Baker Academic Commentary: Matthew, The Seventh Commandment: Divorce*, Baker Publishing, 2007, Matthew 5:31–32, pages 304–305.
138. *The Woman's Freedom to Remarry, Issues Facing Christians Today*, 4th edition, Zondervan Publishing, page 368.
139. Ibid., page 363.

140. Ibid., page 12.
141. Walter A. Elwell, *Evangelical Dictionary of Theology*, "Fornication," Baker Books, 1996, page 422.
142. *Dakes Annotated Reference Bible KJV*, Dake Publishing, Inc., page 315.
143. Ibid., Romans 7:2–3, page 288.
144. Ibid., 1 Corinthians 7:15, page 315.
145. www.mamashealth.com/wedding/presex/
146. www.chicagotribune.com/features/c.
147. Sheila Y. Moore, "Adolescent Boys Are the Underserved Victims of Domestic Violence," *Boston Globe*, December 26, 1999, E7.
148. Jack C. Straton, "What Is Fair for Children of Abusive Men?" *Journal of the Task Group on Child Custody Issues*, 4th ed., Spring 2001.
149. Nancy Nason-Clark, *The Battered Wife: How Christians Confront Family Violence* (Louisville: Westminster/John Knox, 1997), 41, 117.
150. McLean County Domestic Violence, "Safety Planning," http://www.co.mclean.il.us/DV/Safety_Planning.htm.
151. Restraining Orders: Oregon and Washington Domestic Abuse Protection, http://www.divorcenorthwest.com/domestic-violence-attorney.asp.
152. www.christian.org.uk/news/20081031/governmenthasbeen.
153. www.marriagefamilyfoundation.org/consequences-of-the-brea.
154. Ibid., "Impact on Businesses."
155. Ibid., "Impact on Adults."
156. www.divorcereform.org/94staterates.html.
157. *Dakes Annotated Reference Bible KJV*, Dake Publishing, Inc., Proverbs 28:13, page 1103.
158. Ibid., Galatians 6:1, page 360.
159. Ibid., Psalms 51:1, 3, 4, 10, page 944.
160. Wayne A. Mack, *Strengthening Your Marriage*, R & R Press, pages 55–56.
161. *Dakes Annotated Reference Bible KJB*, Dake Publishing, Inc., Ephesians 4:29, page 369.
162. Ibid., Ephesians 5:3–4, page 369.
163. Ibid., Matthew 5:27–28, page 8.
164. Ibid., Philippians 4:8, page 381.
165. Ibid., Ephesians 4:29, page 369.
166. Ibid., Proverbs 18:13, page 1087.
167. Ibid., Proverbs 20:15, page 1090.
168. Ibid., Ephesians 4:29, page 369.
169. Ibid., Romans 15:1–3, page 300.
170. Ibid., Proverbs 15:23, 28, page 1082.

171. Ibid., Proverbs 25:11–12, page 1098.
172. Ibid., Ephesians 4:15, 32, page 368.
173. Ibid., I Corinthians 16:14, page 331.
174. Ibid., Titus 3:1–2, page 424.
175. Ibid., Proverbs 12:25, page 1078.
176. Ibid., Proverbs 3:5–6, page 1066.
177. Ibid., Acts 5:1–11, page 221.
178. www.mamashealth.com/wedding/counsel/
179. Rod I. Huron, *Christian Ministers Manual* (Cincinnati: Standard Publishing, 1984), page 118.
180. www.focusonthefamily.orgtoughlovedrjamesdobson.
181. *2006 National Survey on Drug Use; **Remuda Ranch; ***National Traffic Safety Administration.
182. www.state.sc.us/dmh/bryan/websa.htm.
183. Ibid., "The 12 Steps."
184. http://net-burst.net/guilty/guilt.htmhandlingguiltandshame.
185. Myles Munroe, *Single, Married, Separated & Life After Divorce* (Destiny Image Publishers, Inc., 2003), pages 109–140.
186. www.selfgrowth.com/articles/divorcetoremarriage.
187. M. P. Cosgrove and J. D. Mallory, *Mental Health: A Christian Approach* (Zondervan Publishing, 1977). Stephen M. Huggins, "Traits of a Psychologically Healthy Person," 1999.
188. http://www.stephencovey.com/blog/?tag=the-7-habits-of-highly-effective-families.
189. http://Shannonjordan.blogspot.com/2009/09/whatdoesbiblicalrelationship-look.html.
190. http://Divorcedatingpost.com/content/view/14/321newdatingandyourchildren.
191. www.section21.m6.net/prf-how-php.
192. http://kidproof.blogs.comsamanthawilsoncom/2009/04/eleven-ways-to-spot-apedophile.
193. www.ehow.com/how_134431_blend-families.html.
194. Familylobby.com/printarticle-blendedfamilies:merging2familiesunder one.
195. www.education.com/print/discipline-blended-family.
196. www.ag.org/top/churchworkers/spcl_mfl_marriage.cfm.
197. Ibid., Genesis 2:18, page 4.
198. Ibid., Genesis 1:23, page 2.
199. Ibid., Genesis 1:28, page 2.
200. Ibid., Genesis 2:24, page 4.

201. Ibid., Matthew 19:6, page 36.
202. Ibid., Ephesians 5:22–32, pages 370–371.
203. Ibid., Ephesians 5:30–31, page 370–371.

Glossary

adultery. Voluntary sexual intercourse between a married person and someone other than his or her lawful spouse.

biblical courtship. Also known as *Christian courtship,* this is a term used to denote a particular response to the secular dating culture within various American Christian communities. It involves the oversight of accountability in a person seeking marriage.

blended family. A family composed of a couple and their children from a previous marriage.

cohabitation. To live together as husband and wife, usually without legal or religious sanction.

commitment. The act of committing, pledging, or engaging oneself; a pledge or promise; obligation.

covenant. To promise by covenant; pledge; a binding agreement; the conditional promises made to humanity by God, as revealed in Scripture; the agreement between God and the ancient Israelites, in which God promised to protect them if they kept his law and were faithful to him.

death. End of life; decease, demise, passing, departure; circumstance under which a spouse may remarry another Christian believer.

defraud. To deprive a spouse of sexual relations.

desertion. Willful abandonment, especially of one's wife or husband, without consent or in violation of legal or moral obligations.

divorce. A judicial declaration dissolving a marriage and releasing the husband and wife from all matrimonial obligations.

domestic violence. Acts of violence or abuse against a person living in one's household, especially a member of one's immediate family.

fornication. Any sexual uncleanness or perversity; voluntary sexual intercourse between two persons not married to each other.

marriage. The social institution under which a man and woman establish their decision to live as husband and wife by legal commitments, religious ceremonies, etc.; a covenant relationship between a husband and wife, sanctified in the presence of God and man.

pedophile. An adult who is psychologically distorted in his or her view, believing it is normal to prefer a sexual relationship with a child instead of an adult of the opposite sex; one who seeks out children to fulfill their sexual childhood fantasies.

permanent. Existing perpetually; everlasting, especially without significant change.

perpetual. Lasting indefinitely; continuing or enduring forever; everlasting; continued without interruption.

premarital counseling. A form of counseling that can benefit any couple that is planning to wed each other. Premarital counseling is also called *premarital preparation*.

premarital sex. Sexual intercourse engaged in by persons who are unmarried. It is generally used in reference to individuals who are presumed not yet of marriageable age, or between adults who will presumably marry eventually but who are engaging in sexual activity prior to marriage.

restraining orders. A judicial order to forbid a particular act until a decision is reached on an application for an injunction.

sacred. Entitled to veneration or religious respect by association with divinity or divine things; holy.

safety plan. A safety plan is a plan for how to react to a domestic violence situation. It is decided upon and rehearsed prior to the incident. If you have a safety plan in place and rehearse the plan, it will be easier to react safely to a violent incident.

unbeliever. One who lacks belief or faith, especially in a particular religion; a nonbeliever.

victim. One who is harmed by or made to suffer from an act, circumstance, agency, or condition.

Bibliography

1. Adams, J. E. *Christian Living in the Home.* Phillipsburg, N.J.: Presbyterian and Reformed Publishing Company, 1972.
2. "Bonding and Premarital Sex." (n.d.) www.mamashealth.com/wedding/presex. (Retrieved September 9, 2009.)
3. Covey, Stephen. "Why Happy Families Are Different." (n.d.) http://www.stephencovey.com/blog/?tag=the-7-habits-of-highly-effective-families.
4. Croft, S. "What Does a Biblical Relationship Look Like?" (September 6, 2009). http://Shannonjordan.blogspot.com/2009/09/whatdoesbiblicalrelationship-look.html. (Retrieved October 26, 2009.)
5. *Dakes Annatoted Reference Bible KJV Commentary.* Lawrenceville, Ga.: Dake Publishing, 2006, pp. 36, 333.
6. Dobson, D. J. (2009, September). Tough Love. *Counseling Aids Marriage Succuess*.
7. Downey, C. "How Pedophiles Operate." November 15, 2009. www.section21.m6.net/prf-how-php. (Retrieved November 16, 2009.)
8. Dudley, S. C. "Discipline in the Blended Family." (n.d.) www.education.com/print/discipline-blended-family. (Retrieved October 27, 2009.)
9. Elwell, W. A. *Evangelical Dictionary of Theology.* Grand Rapids, Mich.: Baker Books, 1984, pp. 276, 422.
10. "Fifteen Warning Signs of an Abusive Relationship." (n.d.). www.chicagotribune.com/features/c
11. Hendriksen, W. *New Testement Commentary: Matthew 5:31–32.* Grand Rapids, Mich: Baker Academic, 2007, pp. 304–305.
12. "How to Start Dating Again after Divorce." (n.d.) http://Divorcedatingpost.com/content/view/14/321newdatingandyourchildren (Retrieved November 16, 2009.)
13. Johnson, A. "Are You Ready for Remarriage." (n.d.) www.selfgrowth.com/articles/divorcetoremarriage
14. *Life Application Bible.* Grand Rapids, Mich.: Tyndale House Publishers, 1991, p. 9.
15. *Life Application Bible NIV Commentary: Matthew 19:7–8.* Grand Rapids, Mich.: Tyndale House Publishing, 1991, p. 1691.
16. Mack, W. A. *Strengthening Your Marriage.* R & R Publishing, 1999, pp. 1–3.

17. Regnerus, Mark R. "The Case for Early Marriage." August 16, 2009. *Christianity Today.* http://www.christianitytoday.com/ct/2009/august/16.22.html. (Retrieved October 13, 2009.)

18. McManus, M. J. "Best and Worst Ways to Prepare for Marriage." (n.d.) www.ag.org/top/churchworkers/spcl_mfl_marriage.cfm. (Retrieved October 26, 2009.)

19. Moore, S. Y. "Adolescent Boys Are the Underserved Victims of Domestic Violence." *Study on Children Who Witnesses Domestic Violence.* December 26, 1999, p. E7.

20. Morris, G. "Handling Guilt or Shame." (n.d.) http://net-burst.net/guilty/guilt.htm. (Retrieved October 5, 2009.)

21. Munroe, D. M. *Single, Married, Separated, and Life after Divorce.* Shippensburg, Penn.: Destiny Image Publishers, Inc., 2003.

22. Papalia, D. E. *Human Development, 7th Ed.* Boston: McGraw-Hill, 1988.

23. Phipps, N. "Blended Families: Merging Two Families under One Roof." (n.d.). Familylobby.com/printarticle-blendedfamilies:merging2families underone. (Retrieved October 26, 2009.)

24. *State by State Divorce Rates.* (n.d.). Retrieved from www.divorcereform. org/94staterates.html.

25. Huggins, Stephen M. *Traits of a Psychologically Healthy Person.* 1999.

26. Stott, J. *Issues Facing Christians Today, 4th Edition.* Grand Rapids, Mich.: Zondervan Publishing, 2006.

27. Strong, J. *The Strongest Strongs Exhaustive Concordance of the Bible.* Grand Rapids, Mich.: Zondervan Publishing, 2001.

28. "The Breakdown of Marriage." (n.d.) www.marriagefamilyfoundation. org/consequencesofbreak.

29. *US Census Bureau.* October 23, 1995. www.census.gov/populationusbureauofcensus.unmarried. (Retrieved October 2009.)

30. Whitehead, B. D. "Rethinking Our Commitment to Marriage and Family." (n.d.) http://www.social.jrank.org/pages/891/family-single-parent-households.html.

31. Williams, D. *New Concise Bible Dictionary.* Oxford, England: Lion Publishing, 1898, pp. 337–338.

32. Wilson, S. "Eleven Ways to Spot a Pedophile." April 2, 2009. http://kidproof.blogs.comsamanthawilsoncom/2009/04/eleven-ways-to-spot-apedophile. (Retrieved November 16, 2009.)

33. Writer, e. C. (n.d.). "How to Blend Families." www.ehow.com/how_134431_blend-families.html. (Retrieved October 27, 2009.)